Certificate in Advanced English

Practice Tests

Tony D Triggs

Heinemann English Language Teaching
A division of Heinemann Publishers (Oxford) Ltd
Halley Court, Jordan Hill, Oxford OX2 8EJ

OXFORD MADRID ATHENS PARIS FLORENCE
PRAGUE SÃO PAULO CHICAGO MELBOURNE
AUCKLAND SINGAPORE TOKYO GABORONE
JOHANNESBURG PORTSMOUTH (NH) IBADAN

ISBN 0 435 29484 9 with key
0 435 29483 0 without key

First published 1992

Acknowledgements
This book is dedicated to Bernard Sharp, Internationalist *par excellence*.
The author wishes to thank Kathy Triggs and all those who have trialled these tests.
The Publishers would like to thank Judith Ash, Jacky Newbrook, and Mark Bartram.

We would like to thank the following for permission to reproduce copyright material:
Bison Group (Bison Books Ltd) 'Weather Force' by John Gribbin (p80); Donald Bligh 'What's the use of Lectures' (p51); Extract taken from 'Lateral Thinking' c. Edward de Bono 1970 (p56); Chancerel Publishers extract from Sure Magazine (p78); Churchill 'My Early Life' (Fontana) (p28); Collins Educational (Harper Collins Publishers) 'Transport into the 20th Century' by T. D. Triggs (p59); Consumers Association, 'Fire: Planning an Escape Route and Handy Household Tips' 1983 (p57); 'Product Reviews' Which? Magazine (p49); 'What's Wrong With Cash Machines' Which? Magazine, February 1991 (p69); Foreword to 'The Lochness Story' (Nicholas Witchell) Curtis Brown on behalf of Gerald Durrell c. Gerald Durrell 1974 (p21); G. Firth, History Trail of Bingley – Map (p31); Hoyle and Wrick, 'Diseases from Space' J M Dent and Sons Ltd Pubs (p35); Extracts from 'The RA Expedition' Unwin Hyman of Harper Collins Ltd (p13); Mrs Hoffnung, cartoons from 'Ho Ho Hoffnung' by Gerald Hoffnung (p87); Leeds Churches Community Involvement Project, 'A Neglected Repair' (p33); Text from 'Norfolk Coast and Countryside' and North Norfolk' So Much to See and Do', North Norfolk District Council (p54); the Observer, 'Smile on Gioconda, it Really Was You' by Peter Watson (p67); 'Losing Fat – a Fat-Free Approach' (p12); Pan Books, 'The Walker, the Law and Safety' from 'Walkers Britain', Pan and Ordanance Survey 1982 (p5); Penguin Books Ltd, 'Risinghill: Death of a Comprehensive School' by Leila Berg, Penguin Books 1968 c. Leila Berg, 1968 (p1); 'I'm a busy man' David Myers Cartoon (p20) and 'Boardroom' Blechman cartoon (p66) Punch; Readers' Digest, 'Soya' (p26); Extracts from Safeway nutritional booklets, Safeway Stores Ltd (p74); Tony Soper extracts from, 'Look: Ride a Dolphin: BBC 1969' (p32); George Weidenfeld and Nicholson Ltd, extract from 'Big Business' by C. Northcote Parkinson (p47).

Photographs: Allsport, Gray Mortimore (p89, 93); Bob Martin (p19); Argos (p44); Collections, Brian Shuel (p65); Sally and Richard Greenhill (p92, 43, 86); Robert Harding Picture Library (p88); Impact Photos, Steve Benbow (p91, 95); Rex Features (p90, 94).

Illustrations: Hardlines, Charlbury, Oxfordshire.

Designed and typeset by: Pentacor PLC, High Wycombe, Bucks

Cover design by: Martin Cox

Printed in Great Britain by: Thomson Litho Ltd, East Kilbride, Glasgow

95 10 9 8 7 6 5

CONTENTS

CERTIFICATE IN ADVANCED ENGLISH

INTRODUCTION

This book contains four five-paper tests which imitate as closely as possible the actual tests of the **Certificate in Advanced English (CAE)** examination. The **CAE** has five papers corresponding to those of the **First Certificate in English (FCE)** and **Certificate of Proficiency in English (CPE)** examinations.

They are: **1** Reading
2 Writing
3 English in Use
4 Listening
5 Speaking.

A tape containing the texts for **Paper 4** (Listening) is available separately. The tests are not in order of difficulty, since this would detract from their authenticity; all are as far as possible 'examination identical'.

The **CAE** is a new examination,developed in the light of experience with the **FCE** and **CPE**. The **FCE** caters for a wide range of students, consisting of those who have reached the 'independent user' stage in their English; that is to say, they can cope in English with everyday things like shopping, conversation and writing to friends. At a basic level of competence they are self-sufficient.

Students proceeding to a more advanced level often prepare for the **CPE**. This represents a 'good user' level of attainment, at which students can cope succesfully with college or university courses taught in English. Many go on to pursue such courses though more, of course, take courses in their native language.

People at **CPE** level are approaching the language competence of native speakers, and can go beyond everyday conversation to fluent discussion of abstract topics at quite a deep level. They appreciate details of style and nuance and can choose an appropriate register for what they want to write or say.

Its strengths and characteristics give the **CPE** a special appeal to candidates with an academic or literary bias, and while the **CPE** is an excellent preparation for college or university courses, especially in humanities subjects, it can also serve as a terminal qualification in English for students who are moving on from formal education to work.

The new **CAE** examination is designed, in part, for students in the latter category who would like an alternative qualification better suited to their requirements. The **CAE** is not a test of English for business or other special purposes, but is subtly biased to the testing of skills which could have a practical application. It is easy to illustrate this by reference to the test of refining and proof-reading skills in **Paper 3**. Candidates are required to identify and delete superfluous words in a piece of text. This is a searching test of grammar and comprehension, since superfluous words have a way of suggesting 'decoy' grammars which accommodate them. It is also easy for the eye to miss them, recognising the correct grammar and failing to register items which are extraneous to it. There is nothing overtly vocational in such a test, and the passage used could be drawn – with adaptations – from virtually any source. However, the relevant skill will be most at a premium in the world of work. In real life, it is a document being prepared in an office which is likely to call for refinement and editing – and not, for example, a literary text. The ability to eliminate errors, whether one's own or others', can be of enormous practical use. It also suggests an ability to make first drafts which are more or less error-free.

Other questions, too, test widely-applicable language skills in a practical context. For example, candidates are called upon to amplify notes, paying full regard to achieving a suitable register in the final version.

The choice of texts, especially for **Papers 1** and **4**, will reflect the examination's approach. They will often consist of real-life sources including such things as advertisements, reports and reviews. Some will be adapted as appropriate, while some may appear in 'realia' style. Correspondingly, the writing exercises in **Paper 2** will generally be defined in terms of a clear context, purpose and readership.

The **CAE** represents a standard a little short of **CPE** level. While offering a terminal qualification it can also serve as an intermediate qualification for those progressing from **FCE** to **CPE**. By dividing it into two easy stages the **CAE** makes this major transition less daunting to students.

Whatever the candidates' aim in taking the **CAE** it is hoped that the present book will give them the familiarity and practice they need to achieve success.

ADVICE FOR THE STUDENT

Everyone feels nervous as examination day draws near. Take comfort from the fact that nervousness won't have a big effect on your performance. Language skills don't come and go according to mood or state of mind, and you're sure to get the results you deserve – provided you're familiar with the exam's demands before you take it. These practice tests will help you to gain this important familiarity. They will

a) show you the sort of instructions you'll meet on the real papers. Remember, though, to read the instructions carefully when you're in the exam room – and do exactly as they say.

b) help you to plan your time, learning how to divide it among the various questions. You don't want to finish in a rush; and you don't want to finish far too soon, since this means you haven't taken quite as much care as you should.

Here is some advice and information to help you with each of the five papers.

PAPER 1: READING (1 hour)

This paper consists of four texts selected to test a wide range of reading skills and strategies. The number of questions per text will vary; sometimes there could be two different kinds of questions for one of the passages. The paper includes something which you may not have met in other exams: it asks you to fill the gaps in a passage by choosing from a set of extracts which have been missed out and placed at the end. Begin by reading the whole passage. Try to understand its general shape; in some cases perhaps you can even decide the sort of statement that is missing. Next, read the first of the missed-out extracts. Notice any words at the start that refer back to what has just been said; notice, too, any words at the end that refer to what follows. Let's suppose that the extract begins with the words, 'One thing proved that John was always ready for trouble.' Now look again at the passage and see if there's anything – just before one of the gaps – that goes with John getting into trouble. If so, you've probably found the place where the first extract – A – belongs. Of course, you needn't commit yourself till you've also checked the end of A. Does it lead smoothly into what comes afterwards? If it does then you're almost certainly right about its place in the passage.

Don't be discouraged if A doesn't seem to fit at all. In some questions there are 'spare' answers just to make things more difficult.

Paper 1 is also likely to contain sets of multiple choice questions. You're probably familiar with these, and already know that there's only one correct answer out of the four you are offered. You may be less familiar with questions that ask for matching or filling in. Matching may involve pairing suggested titles with the paragraphs in one of the passages. Filling in is simply a case of writing answers – normally of one word each – in numbered spaces. You will, however, have to decide on the words for yourself, rather than choosing them from a list.

Be sure to read the passages very closely and carefully; answers based on commonsense and general knowledge are fine if you're forced to guess – but they aren't the most reliable way of passing the exam!

PAPER 2: WRITING (2 hours)

This paper falls into two sections, A and B, with equal marks for each. You have to do both these sections. In A you have to do some reading before you start writing. Read the material carefully; it creates the situation and presents the data on which you have to base your answers. There may be something to complain about; perhaps you'll have to give advice or an explanation; perhaps you'll have to apply for a job. The instructions will tell you what to do but you can only do it properly if you study the facts. If there's a job to apply for, these facts may include the advertisement and information about yourself as the imaginary applicant. As you write keep everything clearly in mind – you can always re-read the printed material. And remember to choose a suitable style or 'register' depending on your imagined reader and purpose in writing.

In section B you will have a choice of writing tasks, and this time there will be no material or documents to read – except, of course, the question itself. Read it carefully; as in section A it's important to suit the purpose and audience which are described.

PAPER 3: ENGLISH IN USE (1½ hours)

This paper consists of three sections, A, B and C, carrying equal marks. The total for the paper is approximately 75. There are two different sorts of cloze test in the English in Use paper. The first is in multiple choice presentation; in other words, you are offered a choice of four different answers for each of the gaps. Only one is right and this is the one that – hopefully – you'll mark on your answer sheet. The second cloze test is like the one on the corresponding **FCE** paper. You have to think of the answer yourself without any prompting. There is no list of choices, full of wrong answers to put you off! Just fill the gap in the passage with what you think is the most appropriate word. There could sometimes be alternative answers but in that case they will all be allowed. It is important to write just a single answer, even if you know two or three good ones. (If you do write two or three you are taking a risk; if you get one wrong – even if it's just a spelling mistake – you will lose that particular mark completely. So restrict yourself to the word that fits most simply and easily – often it's just a short, common word.)

Paper 3 includes an exercise where you have to fill gaps with missing material that is given separately. It is rather like the gap-filling test in the Reading paper, but in **Paper 3** the missing material is generally briefer.

Paper 3 also has a question where you have to change the style (or 'register') of a piece of English. This is easier than it sounds, since the second version (usually the more formal one) is presented in a sort of 'skeleton' form, with lots of gaps for you to fill in. You can practise by doing these sample papers but you can also prepare in a more general way, simply by reading and listening as widely as possible. Expose yourself to many different styles of English – and use them, too, when you get the chance. Look for opportunities to give yourself practice. For example, if you've bought something faulty, you can write a grumbling letter to a friend, and also a rather more formal, complaining letter to the shop's head office. Compare the two letters before you post them!

PAPER 4: LISTENING (45 minutes)

This paper is divided into sections, generally consisting of four listening passages.

You may be nervous about this paper. After all, it's true that things that come in the form of sounds have a way of disappearing before you can catch them! However, you can reassure yourself in various ways:

a) Three of the four passages in the test are heard twice.

b) They will all proceed at a relaxed pace—but also in a natural way, where the atmosphere and any background noises are all meant to help you.

c) Each set of questions (which you will have in front of you all the time) will nearly always be in the same order as what you hear on the tape.

d) You can rely on the fact that where you have to put words in boxes *any* right answer will get you a mark. There may be more than one possibility.

The final section is likely to consist of five brief extracts. You will probably have to indicate **two** things about each extract – for example the person's job, **and** what they are talking about. You will do this by ticking or numbering labelled boxes. There will be an extra 10 minutes available for checking answer sheets. The listening tape is available with these practice tests.

PAPER 5: SPEAKING (15 minutes)

This paper consists of four phases, but you will be given a mark for overall performance throughout the paper. The idea of speaking – in exam conditions – for 15 minutes would frighten anyone but in fact the word conversation would cover a large part of what goes on. And in the CAE exam you won't be alone with a single examiner. Instead you'll have a fellow candidate as a partner, and there will be two examiners.

The test will start with informal conversation in which you 'break the ice' and get to know each other a little. Don't prepare for this – or for any part of this paper – by learning a script. It won't sound natural and the examiners won't let you do it for long.

In the next phase the examiner asks you and your partner, in turn, to do some describing, explaining or instructing, normally based on drawings or photographs. By what you say, each of you helps the other to perform some simple task, like selecting a photograph from a set which both of you have in front of you. (You won't be able to see each other's photographs, and they'll be differently arranged on the page, so statements like 'the one in the top left corner' won't be very meaningful.)

Then comes the third phase. Here, you and your partner have to work together to solve a problem or complete a task, probably with a photograph or some other visual item to prompt you. Usually you can agree or agree to disagree. The examiners aren't marking you on the attractiveness of your ideas or whether you reach a particular outcome, but on *how* you interact or collaborate, and the type and range of language you use.

Finally the last phase gives you and the examiners another chance to talk without any pre-ordained pattern. This stage may not be completely informal, since the examiners may wish to focus on the candidate who has had less to say, or about whose mark they are still uncertain. There is justice even for quieter candidates! Remember, though, that if you say next to nothing throughout the paper you cannot be given very high marks! At the other extreme, you may lose marks if you 'swamp' the other candidate and fail to listen or co-operate properly. A good communicator has to listen as well as talk. And don't get carried away and talk too rapidly, as your accent and grammar are likely to suffer.

You are graded on your performance throughout the *whole* of the paper, and not on each individual section. One examiner concentrates on conducting the exam, while the other concentrates on the marking, but you'll all come together at the start and the end. You will be assessed on:

a) speed and rhythm, or fluency of your speech;

b) variety and accuracy of your vocabulary and grammar;

c) quality of your pronunciation. Individual sounds are assessed, and so is the way you link words together;

d) how well you use language to tackle the tasks; for example, how you interact with your partner;

e) how well you interact with your partner.

MARKING

All papers will receive an equal weighting (i.e. 20%).

The **CAE** will be taken in many parts of the world, and papers will be marked by dozens of examiners. Some candidates fear that their work will be marked by an examiner who takes an unfair dislike to their approach, or who simply 'marks low'. This can apply in different degrees to different papers. In some cases marking is very objective; where candidates shade in lozenges (as in **Paper 1**) the marking can even be done by machine. However, many candidates fear that a strong subjective element can apply in the case of other papers, such as **Paper 2**. In practice, this sort of fear is probably inappropriate. Firstly, the paper does not invite free expression, but is designed with great care to test relevance and appropriate style. Secondly, great efforts are made to standardise examiners' marks. Examiners work in teams, and each has its own team leader who – after meeting with other team leaders to decide on standards – will check each examiner's marking and give advice as required.

Finally, a computer check can pick out any high or low marking, or cases where a candidate's marks for a certain paper are out of line with his or her overall standard. No system is perfect, but the Syndicate make sure that theirs is as fair as possible. You do not have to 'pass' every paper; you can make up for one poor paper with a good performance in another.

TEST ONE

PAPER 1 READING 1 hour

FIRST TEXT QUESTIONS 1–8

These questions are based on an extract from a book.

For questions 1–8 you must choose which of the extracts A–I on the following page match the numbered gaps in the text. There is one additional extract which does not belong in any of the gaps. Indicate your answers ***on the separate answer sheet.***

Risinghill – The School, Its Teachers and Its Head

At the time of my visit the staff of Risinghill seemed to me to divide into three; and I suspect they always did.

1	

Because of this, and because they were exceptionally creative people, they were frequently exhausted. They brought to the school their own individual ideas, and their own appreciation of, and pleasure in, the children. They were mature human beings. They would have been an asset anywhere. At Risinghill these child-centred teachers were gold, because they gave equal friendship to children who had known very little of it and only knew adults as enemies.

2	

If anyone were to question the validity of this sacrifice they could not have borne it, for it would have meant that their whole life had been wasted; and who can bear to think of the waste of what will never come again? So they could not stand seeing children saying and doing things that they themselves were never allowed to say or do, or watch them beginning to frame possibilities that for them were crushed in childhood, and not always by other people.

So they told themselves that children should be quiet, that they should be afraid of you, that you should be able to hear a pin drop when you crossed the playground, that children were naturally bad and needed the badness beaten out of them, that individuality must be crushed down by will-power, and that there was satisfaction in this.

3	

And the head, Duane, did not subscribe to this type of 'human' relationship. Such teachers – those in my second category – went their own way. But though they tried to ignore him, the fact that their new head did not approve of the outlook that had hitherto brought them full marks was emotionally exhausting. I have called them the traditionalists, disciplinarians, authoritarians.

4	

They wanted to help him to accomplish his aim. These teachers took Duane's warm spontaneity personally, so that they felt their work was a symbol of a special relationship between them; and when he merely took their work with a quick 'Thanks', or 'Right you are', they felt rejected.

5	

When he showed that on the contrary he expected them to stand on their own feet and make their own decisions, they felt humiliated. In their immaturity and their sudden freedom from the chains – and the certainties – of authoritarianism, these teachers found it very difficult to accept that he expected more strength from them than from the children. They were in a continual state of conflict.

6	

They would describe their philosophic ideas glowingly, so that when you saw what they really did, you were shocked; yet occasionally they actually did what they thought they were doing all the time, like a clumsy child who for a second manages to fit his tracing over the first colourful picture; these moments must have been very satisfying for them, for the children loved them at such times and, generously, forgave and understood a great deal.

7	

And since their varying conduct was based on the unconscious treasuring of Michael Duane as an adult's father figure, they too were exhausted, filled from day to day with frustrations, resentments and anxieties.

8	

For such people did great damage, albeit unintentionally and even quite unconsciously; yet when it was done they were as deeply dismayed as I was.

A These uptight teachers, who depended on emotional support from a head who failed to give it to them, worried me greatly.

B Some teachers were not child-centred at all. Some of these were old and some were not; but they had long ago surrendered their personality, the wishes and beliefs of their own personal life.

C These oppressive teachers placed their faith in a chain of command; they were used to a system where you were told by the person above you, and then you told the person below you.

D But a further section had first been bewildered, and then, under the influence of Michael Duane's personality, decided to try to do what he wanted.

E Some were very good, generous and imaginative. But they were in the minority, and were being fought by other staff as well as by the environment.

F Such teachers thought of themselves as quite different people from the people they really were.

G Simply because Duane did so much, it was easy to assume that he wanted people to lean on him.

H But they would do destructive things and constructive things quite unpredictably.

I The children would only behave if they *supported* the staff; the staff who believed they could rely on force were relying on a fallacy.

SECOND TEXT QUESTIONS 9–18

Answer the following questions by referring to the extract below.

These questions ask you to choose the correct title for each paragraph (1–5). A–H list the possible titles. ***On your answer sheet****, indicate the answer to each question by choosing from the list A–H.*
Note: There is only **one** *answer to each question.*

9	paragraph 1	A	Trouble in Store
10	paragraph 2	B	Football and Society
11	paragraph 3	C	Uncertain Loyalty
12	paragraph 4	D	Pride Restored
13	paragraph 5	E	No Longer the Leaders
		F	Talking Points
		G	Support in Exchange for Advertising
		H	False Hopes

QUESTIONS 9–13

Pleasing The Crowds

1) It is by the results of international fixtures that the status of a country's football is judged. Success in the World Cup, when it was held in England in 1966, induced a kind of euphoria in the minds of football fans who had long felt that the English game was lagging behind that of the Europeans and South Americans. Hungary's defeats of England 6–3 and 7–1 in 1953 and 1954 had made it clear that British soccer could no longer claim to be the best in the world. Not only Europeans, but to an even greater extent the South Americans, showed themselves to be more skilful and imaginative than the English at both international and at club level, and a proliferation of European competitions proved the point beyond all doubt.

2) As the crushing defeats by Hungary in 1953 and 1954 had marked the decline of British football, so the winning of the World Cup in 1966 appeared to mark a period of new supremacy for the victors. However, the next World Cup in 1970, and the subsequent failure even to qualify for the finals in 1974, made it clear that the quality of the English game, with its tactical stereotypes, had fallen behind that of the best of the overseas competition. The repeated claims of managers that the English First Division was the best in the world had failed to convince a public which takes a close interest in the international results, and the fall in gates after the English team failed to qualify in 1974 indicated quite clearly that domestic football is judged in an international context.

3) Despite mixed fortunes in the 1980s the popularity of football in most European countries is fairly high, and the performance of local clubs and national sides is perhaps the most common subject of talk in cafes, clubs and factories. However, the future is not altogether bright. Leading teams like Barcelona and Liverpool enjoy the continued support of loyal fans, irrespective of how individual games turn out on the day, but support for most teams varies from week to week with their fortunes, and future planning in terms of ground development, the provision of amenities and spending in the transfer market is difficult. The impecunious position of some well-known teams is indicative of the danger to even the mightiest of clubs.

4) However, football can also be very big business. Some clubs do take considerable sums at the gates each week. But the really big money comes from sponsors. Sponsors include tobacco companies and car manufacturers. In return for their cash they insist that their name be displayed at the ground, on programmes and on the players' shirts. They also insist on competitions bearing their name; thus even non-smokers have the cigarette company's product on their lips every time they refer to the football scene. Sponsorship helps enormously to stabilise the financial fortunes and standing of clubs. The money is there, even when the results go against them. But they have to beware, since the sponsors will quickly withdraw their support if the downturn in a club's performance lasts for too long. Crowd trouble, too, and the bad publicity this can attract, will drive them away.

5) Bad crowd behaviour, with hooliganism both inside the ground and outside as well, has now become one of football's most disturbing features. As long as football remains 'the people's game' it will reflect current social problems and it might even create a will to resolve them, before they deter increasing numbers of people from attending grounds.

QUESTIONS 14–18

*For questions **14–18** you must choose the answer which you think best completes each unfinished statement about the text. **On your answer sheet** indicate the letter **A**, **B**, **C** or **D** against the number of each question. Give **one answer only** to each question.*

14 In 1966, the result of the World Cup

A was a great achievement for Hungary.
B reflected England's general form.
C gave the English false hopes.
D showed that England had fallen behind other countries in skill.

15 The 1974 World Cup led to

A fewer English people attending football matches.
B managers claiming that English teams were the best in the world.
C the standard of English football falling behind the standard of some other countries.
D people judging teams at home by how they did in foreign countries.

16 According to the passage, when was English football comparatively poor?

A In the 1950s.
B In the 1960s.
C In the 1970s.
D In the 1950s, 1960s and 1970s.

17 The writer says that support for most teams depends on

A the state of the club's finances.
B how well they do in each match.
C how well they plan their spending on their grounds and their teams.
D how well they cope with bad behaviour.

18 Which of the following things does the passage say about sponsorship?

A It leads to non-smokers taking up smoking.
B It leads to competitions being named after cigarette companies.
C It carries on, even if the sponsor's sales do not improve.
D It stops when a club starts to lose its matches.

THIRD TEXT QUESTIONS 19–23

Read this extract from a book about walking in Britain. It is followed by questions or unfinished statements about the text. You must choose the answer which you think fits best. ***On your answer sheet****, indicate the letter* ***A****,* ***B****,* ***C*** *or* ***D*** *against the number of each. Give* ***one answer only*** *to each question.*

The Walker, The Law and Safety

WALKERS' RIGHTS, AND DUTIES

Great Britain has more public footpaths than any nation on Earth. The network in England and Wales is more than 120,000 miles long; in Scotland, where the law is different, walkers theoretically enjoy even more open access to the countryside.

Moreover, in England and Wales, the right to wander the countryside is supported by an interesting principle of law, itself an embodiment of many of the principles of social freedom we take for granted.

If a path is in use without a break for 20 years it is presumed to be a right of way. A landowner can prevent this by closing the path just once during the 20-year period; but the principle, and the possibility, of creating new paths always exists.

A right of way is just what it says: a right of passage across someone's land. The landowner may rightly object if the walker does damage, or leaves litter. But he may not complain – legally – if the walker pauses on the path to enjoy the view, or to eat lunch.

Trespass

If a walker strays from the right of way, he is trespassing. In this case the landowner ought to insist that the trespasser returns to the right of way, or leaves the land. Should the trespasser refuse, the landowner may use the minimum possible force to make the trespasser do so.

It is not an offence, in itself, to trespass; if you are taken to court as a result of trespassing, the landowner will sue for damages. If you, the trespasser, are found guilty, you would pay these damages. They may or may not amount to much in terms of cash; but you would also have to pay the landowner's legal fees: never cheap.

Maintenance

If a public footpath is blocked by wire, machinery, indeed by anything, the landowner is at fault and the walker may go round the obstruction, or climb it, making every effort to cause no damage. Generally, local authorities have a duty to keep the surface of paths in good condition.

A landowner may plough over a footpath if it is not along a field boundary or headland provided the path is returned to usable condition within two weeks of starting to plough, or as soon as practicable if weather prevents this being done. Sometimes farmers leave an unploughed strip; if they do not, the walker is still entitled to walk across, provided he or she keeps to the right of way.

This has tended to be a source of worry and confusion for walkers. People instinctively feel that it is better to trespass, and thereby avoid damage to crops, than to keep to the footpath. But in legal, and practical terms, the best course is to keep to the right of way. The damage to a field under crops is minimal if the walkers keep in single file; the consequences of trespass may be worse.

The Ramblers' Association

All these privileges, which are all too often abused and neglected (especially where ploughing is concerned) are protected on our behalf by the Ramblers' Association.

This is a privately funded lobby group, and if you care about going on country walks, you should support it, too. It has many local branches, some of which helped to prepare this book.

Bulls

Do not let your country walk be spoilt either by being unnecessarily frightened or foolhardy when there are bulls or cows around. Cows and bullocks may rush up to you in a field, but they are rarely being aggressive.

If you see a bull alone in a field where there is a public right of way it is probably there illegally; if it is with cows it is probably there legally. If you encounter a truly aggressive (ie, charging) bull in a field where there is a right of way, tell the police and the Ramblers' Association.

The Landowner
Remember the landowner's point of view, whatever your feelings about private ownership of land. Farmers, rich or poor, provide employment. Possibly their chief objection to walkers centres on dogs, which can upset livestock and kill game. After that, damage to crops and property are the main causes of friction. Share the countryside: you have a right to be there, but it is not exclusive.

SAFETY ON THE HILLS
Britain's mountains and hills are not high, but they are dangerous. Because they are near the sea, their weather changes fast. Much about modern life makes us especially vulnerable to their treachery. We are unfit, because we sit all day. We arrive at walks in the comfort of cars, from which it is doubly hard to imagine the potential nastiness of the serenely inviting hilltops. Once out of the valley, a perfect summer's day can turn, in minutes, to wintry ghastliness.

19 A landowner can

A close a right of way every 20 years.
B use force to stop people trespassing.
C have you fined for leaving litter.
D plough up a footpath at the edge of a field, as long as he makes it usable again.

20 Some landowners object to walkers because

A their dogs damage crops and property.
B they sometimes leave litter.
C they insist on using paths which have been ploughed up and sown with new crops.
D they claim legal rights just because they have used a path for 20 years.

21 Landowners are not generally permitted

A to plough up a right of way across a field.
B to put bulls by themselves on public paths.
C to close routes across their land if the public is starting to use them.
D to use force against walkers who insist on trespassing.

22 If you are out walking and you find that a right of way is ploughed up you should

A find yourself an alternative route.
B walk across the land just the same, even if this means treading on crops.
C keep in single file to avoid trespassing.
D allow time for the path to be put in order.

23 Walks can be spoilt or made dangerous

A by walkers being needlessly frightened of charging bulls.
B by people admiring the view from cars because they are too unfit to do much walking.
C by rapid changes in the weather.
D because hilltops look good from a distance but not close up.

FOURTH TEXT QUESTIONS 24–45

Answer these questions by referring to the magazine article 'Healthy Hobbies' below.

Each question refers to one of the benefits people get from their hobbies, (shown below), and ***A–K*** *list the hobbies themselves.* **On your answer sheet**, *indicate which hobbies give each type of benefit by choosing from the list* ***A–K***.
Note: *Where more than one answer is needed they may be given* **in any order**.

More general knowledge	**24**	**A**	Stamp-collecting
An introduction to foreign languages	**25** **26**	**B**	Writing to pen-friends
Pride in the way things look	**27** **28**	**C**	Gardening
Keeping fit	**29** **30**	**D**	Sport
A chance to compete	**31** **32**	**E**	Authorship
Meeting people	**33** .... **34** .... **35** **36**	**F**	Electronics
Gaining or saving money	**37** **38**	**G**	First aid
Unselfishness	**39**	**H**	Music
Discipline	**40** **41**	**I**	Model-making
Knowledge of science	**42**	**J**	Walking
Habits of being precise and careful	**43** **44**		
Ingenuity	**45**		

Healthy Hobbies

My advice for a long healthy life is to get yourself an absorbing hobby. It's something I can't overemphasise. And the hobbies habit can and should begin in our youth. Hobbies teach us all sorts of things – and they do it in a painless and even pleasurable way. Let me give an example. Stamp collecting is more than just the acquisition of little labels. It's our entry into the whole of world culture and history – at least for the last 150 years. Those little slips of paper celebrate national achievements, reveal conquests and new alliances. The philatelist can learn, too, about currencies, geography, royal houses and all the rest.

Another hobby with obvious overseas links is the cultivation of pen-friends. There are pen-friend agencies which will send your address to potential correspondents in a wide range of countries. And through your letter flap, in the months and years that follow, will come a whole host of interesting letters, sent to you by all sorts of interesting people from remote and exotic places. In the process, if you're a stamp-collector, you gain quite a few choice specimens to add to your collection. And both of these hobbies will give you at least a sprinkling of words from a very wide range of foreign languages.

Some hobbies teach us practical skills or keep us fit. I wouldn't count sport because of all the injuries it can cause. And it can't be continued into ripe old age – not, at least, in the sense of active participation. But keeping fit is most important, so take up walking, and let it mellow into gentle – but still beneficial – gardening as the years progress. Start a child off with a packet of seeds when he's very young, and at 80 he'll be carrying the prize marrow to the horticultural show, and coming home pleased as Punch with his gleaming trophy. As with sport, the competitive spirit is given its outlet. And as a sportsman or an ambitious gardener you'll gain the discipline that comes from learning respect for the judge, the referee or the rule-book. You'll certainly rub shoulders with people and you'll make yourself lots of friends or foes.

Gardening has an added attraction – it can actually help us to make – or at least to save – substantial sums of money. Of course, gardening requisites do have to be bought – at considerable cost – initially; but the fruits of our labours, coming free from the garden, more than repay the initial outlay. Some would claim that an interest in sport is a money-maker too, because of the chance of laying successful and lucrative bets. Personally, it's something I wouldn't encourage. You've more chance of finding a rarity in your stamp collection and selling it for a few thousand pounds; but again I wouldn't encourage excessive optimism. The odds are very much against it.

If you do want a money-making hobby what about authorship? If you've got the skill and application you can write and sell articles to the local and even the national press. On the other hand, if you've got plenty of money and want to spend some there's always photography. If you do your own processing the results will be cheaper than those obtained from your local chemist – but only because you've invested a three- or four-figure sum to equip yourself initially. Some people think that the long periods shut away from the world in their darkrooms make it all worthwhile!

Some hobbies foster a pride in neatness and presentation. Most philatelists want to present their stamps on the album page in the best way possible; and most people writing to pen-friends want their letters to be just as well-presented. Underlying this is the practical need to be understood. I'm assuming that you're conducting the correspondence in your native language and not in your correspondent's language. (Why, oh why, are we so poor at languages? Language-learning could be another hobby if we weren't so lazy.) What was I saying? Oh yes, I was saying that your penfriend is having to cope with what for him or her is a foreign language. Well, then, the least you can do is to make your writing legible, thus ensuring that every letter of every word is a clue to your meaning. Otherwise you're putting extra barriers in the way of international relations!

What about hobbies like chemistry and electronics? I can sum up my views by saying that electric circuits are very unforgiving. One wrong connection and the thing – a radio, a burglar alarm or whatever it is – just won't work at all. And if you go in for chemistry you'll find that bucket analysis – the slap-dash use of excessive amounts of chemicals – won't work either. So as well as teaching us the principles that make the universe tick, these hobbies teach precision – and also a healthy concern for safety. (Which reminds me – studying first aid can be a good hobby too, and it's one that fosters concern for others and offers the chance to meet lots of like-minded, caring people.)

Music is another hobby which teaches us to be exact and attend to fine detail. I used to swap records – as well as stamps – with a girl from Finland, and that led me into performing some rather weird-sounding Finnish music on authentic instruments. It's playing music, not listening to it, that really 'tunes you up', by the way. Instrument-making became the next stage in my long career as a hobbyist; in fact it taught me the sort of ingenuity that can get a ship through the neck of a bottle! There are clubs for construction enthusiasts, so you won't be alone if you do get stuck. Just look upon it as a chance to make friends!

Yes, I can say that my life has been really full and rich, thanks to my hobbies.

TEST ONE

PAPER 2 WRITING 2 hours

SECTION A

You recently bought a railway ticket from Farngrove to your home town, Henley. When planning your journey you consulted a number of timetable leaflets and also the station staff at Farngrove, all of which said that your chosen train would stop at Henley. However, it sped through Henley station and did not stop until it reached Elswood, several kilometres further on. You had your young daughter with you and felt it was too late to go back to Henley by train, since the last bus home from the station would already have left. As a result, though short of money, you took a taxi from Elswood station and sent the receipt to the local railway manager, requesting a refund of the fare. Below is the reply you received, with some handwritten notes which you have made.

Use the letter, the notes and the facts above to write again to the railway office, politely but firmly pressing your claim. You can add any extra details you wish, but do not change any of the information you have been given.

You are advised to write approximately 250 words.

RAILWAY HEADQUARTERS

Loftus Road
Hayleigh
W Yorkshire

14 September 1991

I got on early-couldn't hear them

Dear Sir or Madam

We refer to your claim for a refund of the £18 taxi fare incurred in travelling home from Elswood Station on Tuesday 1st September.

The fact that you had been carried past Henley is most unfortunate, and we apologise for the fact that the timetable leaflet was printed incorrectly. However, we understand from the station master at Farngrove that loudspeaker announcements and platform staff were listing the calling points correctly. Henley was not, of course, mentioned and the fact that the train would not call there should therefore have been quite clear.

Not the person I spoke to!

We should also remind you that tickets are issued on the understanding that we cannot be held responsible for cancellations or delays. Not really relevant

Finally, we would draw your attention to the fact that there are frequent trains from Elswood to Henley; had you travelled back to your home station on one of these you would have avoided the cost of a taxi. Explain about this

But what about the cost!

While we once again apologize for the inconvenience you have suffered you will understand from the points above that we cannot refund your taxi fare.

Yours faithfully

Beryl Bertram

Beryl Bertram

(Passenger Welfare Officer)

SECTION B

Choose **one** *of the following writing tasks. Your answer should follow* **exactly** *the instructions given. You are advised to write approximately 250 words.*

1 A friend has invited you to a party to celebrate a very special occasion in his or her life. Write a letter explaining why you cannot attend. Explain your feelings about the occasion and say how you feel about having to miss it.

2 While on holiday you bought an expensive item. On returning home and trying it out you find that it has a serious fault. You decide to return the item by post. Write a suitable letter to go in the parcel. Explain why you cannot call in person, describe the problem and say what you would like the shop to do about it.

3 You are asked to write a section for a students' guide to eating facilities in your area. You can comment on standard of food, cheapness, convenience, surroundings and anything else you think is relevant. Deal with a single place or compare two or three if you like. The places you choose can be real or invented.

4 A friend is about to come to Britain or your home country to be a student. Write a welcoming letter explaining some of the interesting or important things your friend should know, such as what the weather, food and cost of living are like.

PAPER 3 ENGLISH IN USE 1 hour 30 minutes

SECTION A

1 *Read the article below and for questions* **1–16** *circle the letter next to the word which best fits each space. The first answer has been given as an example.*

SELF DESCRIPTION

So the time has come for you to fill in your college application form. The best advice is to **(1)** . . . that you're the person who's choosing the applicants and to ask yourself what valuable **(2)** . . . you – and you alone – can bring to the college in question. **(3)** . . . every justified opportunity to **(4)** . . . yourself in a positive light. You must **(5)** . . . that you are clear-headed, keen to study your chosen subject – and that you can **(6)** . . . your personality. Make the most of your interests – but bear in mind that any you **(7)** . . . may be probed in depth at interview.

Hopefully, you can **(8)** . . . a deep, thorough interest in one or two fields. Saying you've **(9)** . . . a polar expedition is much more **(10)** . . . than saying you like to go for long walks. If it's true put it down!

Remember to say what your hobbies have taught you. If you **(11)** . . . as a gardener you will surely have **(12)** . . . ideas about the environment. In a similar way, if you're a volunteer hospital porter you'll have gained some significant **(13)** . . . into the needs of the sick and their anxious relatives. Any job may **(14)** . . . deep-seated benefits, even if you undertook it just to earn money.

Getting two or three people to **(15)** . . . your application can be very useful. And make sure your writing is easy for a poor old professor to read. After **(16)** . . . , he may have tired eyes and a hundred other forms to go through.

1	(A) imagine	B presume	C deduce	D intend
2	A elements	B qualities	C factors	D recourses
3	A Catch	B Apprehend	C Have	D Seize
4	A advance	B present	C command	D proffer
5	A show	B manifest	C declare	D display
6	A deliver	B project	C practise	D identify
7	A denote	B boast	C mention	D enumerate
8	A take	B prove	C demonstrate	D reveal
9	A captained	B led	C taken	D undergone
10	A successful	B worthy	C impressive	D illustrious
11	A serve	B work	C labour	D employ
12	A thoughtful	B had	C educated	D informed
13	A awareness	B vision	C understanding	D insight
14	A convey	B confer	C enjoy	D attract
15	A check	B veto	C test	D consider
16	A all	B that	C hours	D yours

2 *Complete the following article by writing the missing words in the spaces provided. Use* ***only one word*** *in each space.*

FUEL FOR THOUGHT

Henry Ford's Model T motor cars appeared on the streets in about 1920. At that time he could have had **(1)** ____________ way of knowing the full effects of **(2)** ____________ he was doing. He was **(3)** ____________ people the new and fundamental freedom **(4)** ____________ personal mobility.

But now we are in a situation **(5)** ____________ half of the world's air pollution comes from car exhausts. Nowhere is this more apparent **(6)** ____________ in America's fume-laden city of Chicago.

But the people of Chicago are not prepared to watch their city choke to **(7)** ____________ . New plans for ridding the area **(8)** ____________ pollutants are well **(9)** ____________ hand. Prohibitive taxes on fuel will restrict the use **(10)** ____________ cars for daily commuting, and car manufacturers will have **(11)** ____________ start making 'cleaner' models. One **(12)** ____________ perhaps there will even **(13)** ____________ cars that suck up polluted air, **(14)** ____________ it as fuel and emit clean air **(15)** ____________ their exhausts.

SECTION B

3 *In most lines of the following text there is* **one** *unnecessary word. It is either grammatically incorrect or it does not suit the sense of the text.*

Read the text, put a line through each unnecessary word and then write the word in the space provided at the end of the line. Some lines are correct. Indicate these lines with a tick (✔) against the line number.

NINE TIPS FOR HEALTHY COOKING

● When you need oil or fat for cooking use vegetable oil,	1	✔
not butter or lard. And use as ~~is~~ little as possible.	2	is
● When you buy a meat buy the leanest cut you can afford.	3	
And cut off obvious bits of excess of fat before you start	4	
cooking. When you use mince, bear it in mind that it	5	
is probably much more fatty than it looks. Heat it, then	6	
add cold water and you skim off the floating fat. ● Stewing	7	
is healthy, and once again you have the added in advantage	8	
of being able to spoon off the fat before the serving.	9	
And use beans and pulses to replace for some of the meat	10	
in your stews. ● When you cook poultry, remove some or	11	
all of the skin off. ● When you cook fish, grill or	12	
bake it instead of frying it. Particularly must avoid	13	
deep-frying it in batter. ● Make sauces with cornflour	14	
and instead of using the roux method. ● Serve baked or	15	
boiled potatoes rather than serve chips; and don't add	16	
butter either to beans or to any other vegetables either.	17	

4 *You are a clerk at a printing works and have just received the following informal note from one of your colleagues. Using the information given complete the formal letter to the customer by writing the missing words in the spaces provided on the right. Use* **not more than two words** *in each space.*

What with the weather etc. Mr Miller's leaflets aren't ready yet. Mr Jenkins from production says it can't be helped — he had no electricty during the snowstorm, and very few staff. Anyway, they're getting on with the leaflets now, and Mr Jenkins will ring Mr Miller before the end of this month to let him know how the work is going.
The job should be done by the middle of September and we'll send the leaflets to Mr Miller then. We'll just have to say we're sorry and hope the delay isn't putting him out too much.

(1) . . . adverse weather and other **(2)** . . . there has been an unfortunate but **(3)** . . . **(4)** . . . in producing your leaflets. The recent heavy snow caused a **(5)** . . . failure and a very high level of **(6)** . . . among our staff. We are now giving your leaflets top **(7)** . . . and we will ring you at the end of the **(8)** . . . month to **(9)** . . . you of **(10)** . . . . The work should be **(11)** . . . by **(12)** . . . , and the leaflets will then be **(13)** . . . as quickly as possible. We must once again offer our sincerest **(14)** . . . and trust that the delay will not cause you too much **(15)**. . . .

1	*owing to*	8	
2		9	
3		10	
4		11	
5		12	
6		13	
7		14	
		15	

SECTION C

5 *Choose the best phrase or sentence (given below the text) to fill each of the blanks in the following text. Write one letter (***A – G***) in each of the numbered spaces. Two of the suggested answers do not fit at all.*

ANCIENT WANDERERS

When was America discovered? Nobody knows. The first people to set foot on American soil had no way of calculating time. They had no calendar. They could not write. Their geographical concepts were too limited for them to realize that they had reached a new continent.

(1) __________ , and they spent their lives, like their forefathers, roaming the frozen coasts of Arctic Siberia, until one fine day they found themselves on the eastern shore of the ice-covered Bering Strait. **(2)** __________ .

We do not know if they had walked across frozen water, or paddled with their crude fishing tackle in a frail craft along the naked shore of tundra and snowdrifts. Nor do we know when their descendants began to spread southward through Alaska and down through the whole of North, Central and South America. **(3)** __________ , but this view is not universally held. All agree, however, that the first steps into America were taken in prehistoric times.

(4) __________ , and recent discoveries indicate that primitive family groups continued to move back and forth between Siberia and Alaska. Inside America, from Alaska in the north to Tierra del Fuego in the south, the rising generation settled in igloos, in wigwams, in leaf huts and in caves. **(5)** __________. Thus a long chain of highly distinct Indian tribes began to develop inside America. Not only did they differ strikingly from one another in facial type and body build, but they spoke quite unrelated languages and evolved completely different ways of life.

A Finding homes was of course extremely important

B Some believe that it was about 17,000 years ago

C The narrow gap between Arctic Asia and Alaska was always passable

D They could not have suspected that only Arctic animals had roved here before them

E Others continued to live in Siberia

F The key to success lay in quick adaptation to local conditions

G They were homeless, nomadic hunters and fishermen

6 *You have been asked to write a short article for a student newsletter giving some practical advice about complaining after buying faulty goods.*

You have made some initial notes on which to base your article. You must use all the words in the same order they appear in the notes. You may add words and change the form of words where necessary. The first point has been expanded for you as an example.

Sensible shopping

a Secret of successful shopping – time to check/examine thoroughly.

b Also important: save receipt – never certain fault not crop up later. Example: new table lamp burst into flames when try it out!

c Receipt: what, where, when bought, how much. If have to complain take back to shop.

d Remember law: shop put right, not manufacturer.

e If suggest you send back to maker refuse.

f If say will send back to maker themselves ask immediate refund.

g If serious trouble: calm, polite. Leave shop, write head office. Explain in detail – remember right to compensation if injury, damage.

Sensible shopping

For many new students at Camberton International Centre, shopping in England will be a wholly new experience. Fortunately, English law protects the shopper fairly well, and many shops are positively eager to live up to the laws's demands. They know that their reputation depends on it. Of course, it's still up to you to take care and try to protect your own interests.

a The secret of successful shopping is to allow enough time to check and examine the things you're buying thoroughly.

b ____

____

____

c ____

____

____

d ____

____

____

e ____

____

____

f ____

____

____

g ____

____

____

Well, after all that, let me just wish you happy and trouble-free shopping in England. It can be and often is a pleasure. The commonest problem is lack of money, not faulty goods. But if, as students, we're short of money, there's all the more reason to use it carefully.

TEST ONE

PAPER 4 LISTENING 35 minutes

SECTION A

Look at the railway map and sentences 1–9.

You will hear a radio travel bulletin. As you listen you should use the information in the bulletin to complete the sentences. You will hear the piece ***twice.***

1 The bulletin is for passengers on the __________ Region of British Rail.

2 According to the bulletin, the recent __________ have caused __________ and __________ while in the Newmarket area __________ have occurred.

3 Services to and from Diss are being provided __________________ .

4 The advice for passengers to London is to avoid __________ and ______________ instead.

5 Getting from Norwich to Ipswich involves ______________________________ .

6 British Rail will try to ensure that if passengers have to make extra changes ______________ .

7 Some journeys from Cambridge to Ipswich will take __________ minutes longer than usual because ______________________________ .

8 The service from Ely to Ipswich should be ______________________________ .

9 Services from North Walsham to the __________ are being provided by coach. Passengers from Cromer to Norwich should ______________________________ .

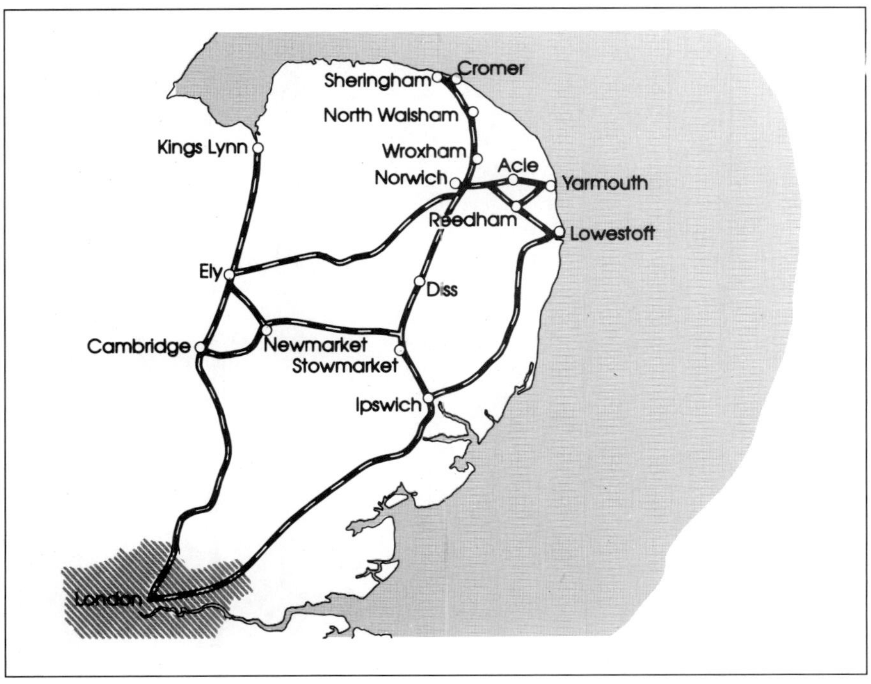

SECTION B

10 *You will hear two people discussing what they need to buy at the start of their holiday. As you listen tick the boxes that correspond to the things that one of the people, John, is expecting to get.*

Listen carefully as you will hear the piece ONLY ONCE.

Orange juice	☐	Spring onions	☐
Tea or coffee	☐	Beetroot	☐
Milk	☐	Salad cream	☐
Cornflakes	☐	Tinned beans	☐
Porridge oats	☐	Spaghetti	☐
Bread	☐	Tomato Sauce	☐
Marmalade	☐	Cheese	☐
Butter	☐	Sweets and chocolate	☐
Margerine	☐	Throat sweets	☐
Matches	☐	Peanuts	☐
Washing up liquid	☐	Chewing gum	☐
Soap	☐	Crisps	☐
Washing powder	☐		
Grapes	☐		
Tomatoes	☐		
Olives	☐		
Celery	☐		
Lettuce	☐		

SECTION C

You will hear a doctor and a professor speaking in public about how to study successfully. For questions **11–27**, *complete the notes using a few words; you do* **not** *need to write full sentences. You will hear the piece* **twice.**

Professor Jenkinson thinks habits are useful because

they | **11** | . |

There are three habits students need to acquire:

- They should get in the habit of working | **12** | . |
- They should get in the habit of working | **13** | . |
- They should get in the habit of having plenty of | **14** | . |

and | **15** | |

Dr Murphy suggests that listening to music through

earphones | **16** | | but he suggests that it might be good

for the students' | **17** | . |

The Professor thinks that before students | **18** | | they

should | **19** | | the table where they work. They should not

leave anything | **20** | | on it.

Dr Murphy thinks that students need at least | **21** | | to

do a useful amount of work.

Professor Jenkinson thinks students need a period of | **22** | |

if they are going to study part of a textbook in a serious way.

Learning | **23** | | should be done in 20– or 30– minute spells.

Students need to be at their freshest for | **24** | |

or | **25** | . |

For the non-athletic Dr Murphy recommends | 26 | . |

The Professor thinks that | 27 | | study is more important

than | | . |

SECTION D

You will hear various people talking about how they spend their evenings.

TASK ONE lists their pastimes or activities. Put them in the order in which you hear them by writing a number from 1–5 in each box. Three boxes will remain empty.

TASK 1

Running	28	
Swimming	29	
Watching television	30	
Working as a cleaner	31	
Cycling	32	
Enjoying the countryside	33	
Painting and decorating	34	
Long-distance walking	35	

TASK TWO lists the people you hear speaking in the five extracts. Put the speakers in the order in which you hear them by writing a number from 1–5 in each box. Three boxes will remain empty.

You will hear the series twice.

TASK 2

Gardener	36	
Artist	37	
Typist	38	
Messenger	39	
Labourer	40	
Shop assistant	41	
Cleaner	42	
Taxi driver	43	

TEST ONE

PAPER 5 SPEAKING 15 minutes

QUESTION 1 (candidate 1)

The examiner will ask you to describe the photograph on page 88 to your partner, who has a photograph which is related to yours in some way.

At the end of one minute the examiner will ask your partner to say what the relationship between your pictures is. You should then try to reach agreement with your partner.

NB: The instructions would not appear on the examination material in the real exam. They would be conveyed orally by the examiner.

QUESTION 1 (candidate 2)

The examiner will ask your partner to describe a photograph to you. The photograph on page 92 is related to your partner's in some way.

After one minute you may ask short questions if you wish or find it necessary. The examiner will then ask you to say what the relationship between the photographs is. You should then try to reach agreement with your partner.

QUESTION 2 (candidate 1)

The examiner will ask your partner to describe one of the six photographs below to you.

At the end of one minute the examiner will ask you to say which photograph your partner was describing.

QUESTION 2 (candidate 2)

The examiner will ask you to describe one of the six photographs below to your partner (who has the same six photographs).

At the end of one minute the examiner will ask your partner to say which photograph you were describing.

QUESTION 3 (both candidates)

"I'm a busy man—what can I do for you?"

Look at the cartoon.

Discuss with your partner what it says about the man at the desk. What serious point is it making about the world of work or the world of business? You must either reach agreement or 'agree to disagree'. Make sure that you understand your partner's opinion. At the end of three minutes you will be asked to report your decision to the examiners, and take part in further discussions.

TEST TWO

PAPER 1 READING 1 hour

FIRST TEXT QUESTIONS 1–7

These questions are based on an extract from a book.

For questions 1–7 you must choose which of the extracts **A–H** *on the following page match the numbered gaps in the text. There is one additional extract which does not belong in any of the gaps.*

Indicate your answers ***on the separate answer sheet.***

Persistent Doubters

It has always seemed very curious to me that many people, faced with reasonably good evidence as to the existence of a creature as yet unknown to science, maintain an air of the utmost doubt and scepticism. Why should they not throw up their hands in delight at even the faintest chance of such a windfall in this shrinking world?

Unfortunately, people whose intelligence you had no cause to doubt suddenly leave you bereft of speech at the length to which they will go to prove that nothing new can exist under the stars.

1	

Since that date, there has been an endless succession of equally arrogant individuals who adopt the same blinkered attitude.

2	

The strange psychology underlying people's excessive scepticism is one of the most intriguing facets of the story. It is indeed a puzzling reflection on our purportedly rational civilisation that the testimony of so many reliable witnesses, often offered under oath, should have been considered inadequate as proof that there is something unknown in the Loch.

3	

What I am advocating is a reasonably open mind. There are after all plenty of strange things in the world which we now accept but were once dismissed as ridiculous and impossible fantasies. Think of the courage it must have taken to set out to describe the first duck-billed platypus.

4	

Yet they have only to travel to New Zealand, where they will find the tuatara which has come down from the pleistocene age unchanged. And this is not the only survivor: the coelecanth could not be more prehistoric if it tried.

5	

So let us no longer take refuge behind a barricade of leaping salmon, shadows, dead stags, logs of wood, branches and acrobatic otters. Instead, let us have the courage to admit that there is something large, strange and unknown to science in the cold waters of the Loch.

6	

You would have thought that British tourist authorities would have backed to the hilt any expedition designed to track down and identify the Loch Ness phenomenon.

7	

He wrote that if medical science had shown as little enterprise and as little courage as marine biologists have shown then tuberculosis would still be killing millions in Europe every year.

A So many people state that a prehistoric monster (that contradictory term beloved of the press) could not exist today.

B I am not suggesting for a moment that one accepts the existence of an unknown creature without sifting the evidence with great care.

C The saga of the Loch Ness Monster makes fascinating reading.

D It seems incredible that all the research to date has been done on a shoe string by dedicated amateurs who, when they were helped at all, received assistance from America and only scorn from the ranks of British science.

E It would be a sad comment on human beings if a creature that had survived for so long died out due to human pollution before its existence was even acknowledged.

F Mr Philip Stalker, writing about the Monster in 1975, made a harsh but justified comment.

G It was the scientist Cuvier who produced the arrogant statement that there were no new large animals to be discovered, for he knew them all.

H Time and again we hear of intelligent witnesses who are told by scientists that they are drunk, insane, partially blind or at best clever hoaxers.

SECOND TEXT QUESTIONS 8–33

Answer these questions by referring to the text 'Worlds Apart', which begins below.

Questions 8–19 ask you about conditions on some of the planets. ***On your answer sheet****, indicate your answers to these questions by choosing from the list* ***A–K*** *(shown below).*

Note: *Where more than one answer is needed you may give the answers in any order.*

According to the passage:	**A** too cold
Why can no one live on Pluto? **8** **9**	**B** no atmosphere
Why can no one live on Neptune **10** **11**	**C** always dark
What do Jupiter, Saturn, Uranus and Neptune have in common? **12** .... **13** .... **14** **15**	**D** poisonous atmosphere **E** atmosphere made of carbon dioxide
Why is Venus so hot? **16**	**F** very near sun
Why is Mercury so hot? **17**	**G** rings
What special features does Saturn have? **18** **19**	**H** liquid poison
	I no living things
	K very large

Worlds Apart

From early childhood the solar system fascinated me almost more than words can tell. My interest began near to home, as it were. I saw from my window trees, soil and distant hills, and in a gap between the hills a curving line where the sea met the sky. But why a *curved* line, I asked myself. I began to understand that the world was a giant ball, tumbling, forever tumbling round our local star. And soon I discovered, mainly from books, that the world has brother and sister worlds, which also attend the sun on its travels.

One night – I think I must have been seven – an uncle pointed to a bright red blob among the stars. 'That's Mars,' he said, 'It's one of the planets.'

I was thrilled. This was my first conscious sighting of Mars.

'Is it hot?' I asked. 'It looks red hot.'

'No,' said my uncle. 'It's colder than our world.'

'Why is it colder?'

'Well it's further from the sun than our world. And it hasn't got as much air around it.'

'Is it the coldest planet of all?'

My lecturer uncle was in his element! 'Oh no,' he replied. 'There's Jupiter – that's the next one from Mars. Then there's Saturn, Uranus, Neptune and Pluto. Pluto's the furthest of all from the sun.'

'So when they sit in the sun on Pluto they freeze to death!' For some strange reason I thought my remark was really funny. 'Those poor Plutonians,' I chuckled. 'Oh those poor Plutonians.'

It was then that my uncle unthinkingly gave me the greatest mental shock of my childhood. 'There's no one on Pluto. It's far too cold and there isn't any air to breathe.'

'No one there?' I echoed in total disbelief. 'But there must be people.'

'How could there be? It's frozen solid. It's so far away from the sun that it's always dark there.'

'Even in the day?'

'Yes, if you went to Pluto and looked at the sun you'd just see a very bright star. The sky would be black and full of stars and the sun would just be the brightest one.'

I was amazed – and eager to know about *all* the planets. 'So if I came back from Pluto towards the earth which planet would I get to first?'

'Well, first you'd bump into Neptune – bigger than Pluto, bigger than our world and covered in swirling, poisonous clouds.'

'Poisonous clouds?'

'Yes, poisonous ones – and you'd never see the sky or the sun at all. They're so terribly thick.'

'And what about people? Are there people on Neptune?'

'Oh no, there's no people or animals. This here is the only place where there's life so far as I know.' My uncle tapped his foot on the ground.

'So Neptune's too cold?'

'That's right – so are all the giant planets. And that means all the planets as far as Jupiter.'

In my mind I surveyed my homeward journey from the outer edge of the solar system. Little dead Pluto and then the dead giants. Feeling forlorn, I clutched at the only straw I could. 'But don't they even have good air?'

'No,' said my uncle. 'Just poisonous clouds.'

'Poisonous clouds,' I marvelled for the second time that night.

This time my uncle must have sensed the puzzled reproach in my voice. 'Ok I'll explain,' he offered, eager as ever to show off his learning. 'You know when you go to the dentist and he puts you to sleep with his special gas. Well, the clouds on some of the planets are made of the same sort of stuff. Not exactly the same, but no good for breathing.'

'So I'd fall asleep.'

'You wouldn't just fall asleep. You'd die, if you weren't dead already.'

My uncle was getting carried away, but so was I. 'Did you tell me once about Saturn being covered in seas of poison?'

'Yes, that's right. And you wouldn't believe me when I said you'd be too heavy to stand up straight on Jupiter.'

'I still don't believe you.'

'It's all to do with gravity. Mars, of course, is smaller, so the gravity's less. You could jump right over a house on Mars. Although, of course, there aren't any houses,' he added hastily. 'But there is some air – a bit like the air we're breathing now, but very thin. You'd see the sun and you'd feel its warmth.'

'So I could do things on Mars – like going swimming, and that sort of thing.'

'No, it's too cool for that. And there's not enough water. It never rains or snows on Mars and there aren't any seas or rivers or lakes. You'd see frost on the ground in the morning and there might be just enough sun to melt it during the day – but only just. Anyway, you'd have a hard job swimming in a space suit, you know.'

'And I'd need it to give me proper air. But what about food? Do plants grow on Mars?'

'Well, there might be some moss or something like that. But you'd best get right back to earth if you want a really good meal. Or if you needed warming up you could fly right past our world and carry on to Venus or Mercury. Look – there's Venus; just above Mrs Jackson's house.'

I looked along my uncle's pointing arm. And there it was – a silver light almost resting on our neighbour's roof and seeming ready to pop down her chimney.

'It looks really big.'

'It's only about the same size as our world. It's bright because it's covered in clouds and it's near to the sun. What you can see is sunlight bouncing off the tops of the clouds.'

'And are the clouds poisonous?'

'Not exactly. They're made of a gas called carbon dioxide. *We* breathe it out and plants breathe it in. If they didn't do that there'd be too much of it. Then it would trap the sun's heat and make the world too hot. And there *is* too much on Venus. So the heat would kill you – even if you kept your space suit on. But it's even hotter on Mercury. That's the last little world you'd come to before the sun's heat turned your spaceship into a puff of smoke! Even on Mercury it's hot enough to melt some of the metal. There's no air or clouds to trap the sun's heat. Little worlds like Mercury and Pluto just can't hold on to any atmosphere. But the sun's very near to Mercury, and it's blazing away like a painter's blowlamp.'

'So there aren't any creatures on Venus – or on Mercury.'

'I'm afraid there aren't.'

My disappointment – my cosmic loneliness – was complete. But I owe to that elderly uncle, long since dead, my lifelong interest in astronomy. I know it sounds ridiculous, but nowadays, when I turn my telescope on the planet Saturn, haloed with its beautiful rings, I always think of that saintly and amusing man who taught me so much.

*Questions **20–33** ask you to name the appropriate planet or planets.* **On your answer sheet,** *indicate your answers to these questions by choosing from the list* ***A–H.***

According to the passage:

Which planet looks hotter than it really is?	20		
Which planets does the boy see in the sky?	21	22	
Which planets have no atmosphere?	23	24	
Which planets have stronger or weaker gravity than the earth's?	25	26	
Which planets are very small?	27	28	
Which planet, apart from the earth, might have plants?	29		
Which are the two nearest planets to Pluto?	30	31..........	
Which planet has poisonous clouds which would hide the sun?	32		
Which planet is a similar size to the earth?	33		

A Jupiter
B Mars
C Mercury
D Neptune
E Pluto
F Saturn
G Uranus
H Venus

THIRD TEXT QUESTIONS 34–38

Read the following extract from a magazine and answer questions 34–38.

Soya

Anne Ager, well-known food journalist, introduces you to a selection of delicious healthy flavours, all prepared with soya oil or margarine . . . dishes that are ideally suited to specific meals throughout the day.

We are now more aware of healthy eating than ever before. We understand the beneficial and harmful effects that certain foods can have on our bodies, and we tend to buy and cook accordingly. So just what are the food facts that we have learnt over the past few years?

Saturated fats, animal fats such as butter, tend to be bad for us, whereas polyunsaturated fats such as those found in soya oil are much healthier. The body needs two essential fatty acids, linoleic and linolenic, both of which are found in soya oil. ● Reduce overall fat content in drinks and cooking by using skimmed milk instead of full fat milk ● Use creme fraiche or natural yoghurt instead of cream ● Use healthier cooking methods e.g. grill foods with soya margarine, or stir fry with soya oil ● Reduce salt intake slightly and add flavour to foods by using herbs and spices ● Cook vegetables very lightly, or preferably, use them raw ● Reduce portion sizes or regularity of eating red meat . . . eat more fish and 'white' meat such as poultry ● Sweeten desserts naturally with fruit, rather than adding sugar.

WHAT IS SOYA? . . . WHERE DOES IT COME FROM?

The soyabean, the fruit of the soya plant, is one of the oldest vegetables known to man. Although it was cultivated as staple food in the Far East long before historical records existed, soya was not introduced into Europe and America until the 18th century. 60% of the world's soyabean production is now grown by American farmers.

Foods that originate from the soyabean are highly nutritious, being rich in protein, fibre, essential oils, minerals and vitamins: soya milk, soya flour, soyabean curd, soya sauce, and soya oil and soya margarine.

Soya oil is obtained by dividing the oil out of the beans and then purifying it. Soya margarine, which is high in polyunsaturates and has a pleasant, light flavour, is made by blending liquid soya oil with hydrogenated 'solid' soya oil.

TASTE OF SOYA MENUS

The healthy flavours that we have already talked about have been brought together with soya margarine and soya oil, to give daily healthy menus for 7 days.

The menus are suitable for all the family, and substitutes can be made if a particular ingredient is not liked i.e. one variety of fish can be swapped for another.

Lunch and dinner on any one day are interchangeable, so as to fit in with the activities of your day.

GENERAL HEALTHY GUIDELINES:

● Spread soya margarine sparingly on bread or toast ● Use skimmed milk in tea or coffee (preferably no sugar) – keep both tea and coffee to the minimum ● Avoid most spirits and drink wine sparingly ● Drink fresh fruit juices or mineral water in preference to sweetened juices and fruit cordials ● Eat wholemeal bread or wholegrain bread no more than 2 slices per day ● Nibble on raw vegetables and fruits rather than high calorie between-meal snack foods, such as crisps or biscuits.

*For questions **34–38** you must choose the answer which you think best completes each unfinished statement about the text.* **On your answer sheet**, *indicate the letter* **A**, **B**, **C** *or* **D** *against the number of each question. Give* **one answer only** *to each question.*

34 The extract is

A part of an article about healthy eating.
B the introduction to a set of suggested meals in a magazine.
C part of an advertisement.
D part of an article about soyabeans and soya products.

35 The dishes Anne Ager recommends are to be prepared

A either with or without soya products.
B with soya products only.
C with less salt and more herbs.
D by grilling or stir-frying.

36 Our buying and cooking habits are influenced

A by the wish to eat food which tastes good.
B by the part of the world we live in.
C by the need for convenience.
D by concern over health.

37 For the sake of our health we should

A swap one kind of fish for another.
B substitute fish and poultry for certain other kinds of meat.
C drink fruit cordials rather than coffee or tea.
D use plenty of soya margarine on our bread or toast.

38 Soya margarine is

A enriched with nutrients.
B made with polyunsaturated fats.
C made from liquid and solidified soya oil.
D given a delicate, pleasant flavour.

FOURTH TEXT QUESTIONS 39–48

Answer the following questions by referring to the extract below.

These questions ask you to choose the correct title for each paragraph (1–6). A–I list the possible titles. On your answer sheet, indicate the answer to each question by choosing from the list A–I.

***Note:** There is only one answer to each question.*

39	paragraph 1	**A**	Revenge
40	paragraph 2	**B**	Mixed Success
41	paragraph 3	**C**	Frightening Facts
42	paragraph 4	**D**	Making Peace
43	paragraph 5	**E**	A Chance Hit
44	paragraph 6	**F**	Bad Luck and Good Luck
		G	Giving Way to Temptation
		H	Picking on Someone the Wrong Size
		I	On the Brink of Success

First Days at Harrow

1) I first went to Harrow in the summer term. The school possessed the biggest swimming-bath I had ever seen. It was more like the bend of a river than a bath, and it had two bridges across it. We used to go there for hours at a time, and bask between our dips, eating enormous buns, on the hot asphalt margin. Naturally it was a good joke to come up behind some friend, or even enemy, and push him in. I made quite a habit of this with boys of my own size or less. One day when I had been no more than a month in the school, I saw a boy standing in a meditative posture wrapped in a towel on the very brink. He was no bigger than I was, so I thought him fair game. Coming stealthily behind, I pushed him in, holding on to his towel out of humanity, so that it should not get wet.

2) I was startled to see a furious face emerge from the foam, and a being evidently of enormous strength making its way by fierce strokes to the shore. I fled; but in vain. Swift as the wind my pursuer overtook me, seized me in a ferocious grip and hurled me into the deepest part of the pool. I soon scrambled out on the other side, and found myself surrounded by an agitated crowd of younger boys.

3) "You're in for it," they said. "Do you know what you have done? It's Amery; he's in the Sixth Form. He is Head of his House; he is champion at Gym; he has got his football colours." They continued to recount his many claims to fame and reverence, and to describe the awful retribution that would fall upon me. I was convulsed not only with terror, but with the guilt of sacrilege. How could I tell his rank when he was in a bath-towel and so small?

4) I determined to apologise immediately. "I am very sorry," I said as Amery closed in upon me. "I mistook you for a Fourth Form boy. You are so small." He did not seem at all placated by this; so I added in a most brilliant recovery, "My father, who is a great man, is also small." At this he laughed, and after some general remarks about my "cheek" and how I had better be careful in the future, signified that the incident was closed. I have been fortunate to see a good deal more of him, in times when three years' difference in age is not so important as it is at school. We were afterwards to be Cabinet colleagues for a good many years.

5) It was thought incongruous that while I apparently stagnated in the lowest form, I should gain a prize open to the whole school for reciting to the Headmaster twelve hundred lines of Macauley's "Lays of Ancient Rome" without making a single mistake. I also succeeded in passing the preliminary examination for the Army while still almost at the bottom of the school. This examination seemed to have called forth a very special effort on my part, for many boys far above me in the school failed in it.

6) I also had a piece of good luck. We knew that among other questions we should be asked to draw from memory a map of some country or other. The night before, by way of final preparation, I put the names of all the maps in the atlas into a hat and drew out New Zealand. Thereupon I applied my good memory to the geography of that faraway country. Sure enough the first question in the paper was: "Draw a map of New Zealand." This was what gamblers call an *en plein*, and I ought to have been paid 35 times my stake, novice and Third Form boy that I was. However, I certainly got paid very high marks for my paper.

[From *My Early Life* by Sir Winston Churchill]

QUESTIONS 45–48

Questions 45–48** are a number of questions or unfinished statements about the text. You must choose the answer which you think fits best.* ***On your answer sheet *indicate the letter* **A**, **B**, **C** *or* **D** *against the number of each question. Give* ***one answer only*** *to each question.*

45 Churchill thought Amery was a good person to push into the water

A because they already knew each other.
B because Amery was the right size.
C because Amery had a towel to keep him warm afterwards.
D because of the way Amery was standing at the edge of the pool.

46 What was the first thing Churchill learned about the person he had pushed into the water?

A His anger and strength.
B His importance.
C His speed.
D His name.

47 Churchill's excuse for what he had done was

A very clever.
B tactless.
C amusing to Amery.
D meant to be cheeky.

48 Churchill was lucky in his Army entrance examination because

A his memory was good.
B he correctly guessed that there would be a question about New Zealand.
C he had studied New Zealand at the last minute.
D the examiners seemed to take account of his youth.

TEST TWO

PAPER 2 WRITING 2 hours

SECTION A

You work for a newspaper and you spent your recent holiday visiting a friend in the Yorkshire town of Bingley. The diary (written during your visit) and the letter (written shortly afterwards) show what you thought of Bingley at the time. Now your editor has asked you to write an article for the newspaper's regular series 'Round and About', which introduces towns and tourist attractions.

Use the diary, letter and map to help you to write your article, which should be about 250 words in length. You do not need to include all the information and should **not** *describe your own holiday. You may add any extra details to complete your answer, provided that you* **do not change** *any of the information given.*

Sat	Bad start: train late and station dreary – very near shops and cafes though! Tired so lazy afternoon in Myrtle Park. Smell of roses and freshly-cut grass. John says visit other park tomorrow – pine trees, squirrels etc., old quarry.
Sun	Yes, lovely park but what a climb! Looked down on valley. Could hear brass band.
Mon	Went shopping in Main Street. Saw church and old houses. Too much traffic thundering through.
Tues	Rain, rain, rain, and not much to do. Bought fish and chips and ate them under bandstand in park – v. good shelter! Cafe, tennis courts open, but v. short of customers.
Wed	Nice country walk along Beckfoot Lane, Cross Gates Lane and Altar Road. Millgate busy but riverside nice. Saw a couple of swans. Angered fisherman by tripping over rod! Winding roads from river to canal (lots of holiday barges – must try it next year) and back to the shops along the bank. Big meal at John's house.
Thurs	Back up Park Road to historical buildings. Not my cup of tea but didn't tell John. Afternoon in Bell Bank Wood. Wildlife galore. View of valley. Rumble of traffic.
Fri	Lazy day. Packing in evening. Sad to go home, would love to stay longer. Noise of traffic and birds (including John's hens) from 4am so don't need alarm clock.

Elton Lodge
Newley
Norfolk

Thursday 1 August

Dear John,

Thank you for a lovely holiday. The station didn't look so bad in the sunshine, and I hope I'll be seeing it – and you – again very soon.

We were so busy getting out and about that I never gave you my honest opinion about the town. Don't be offended, but I can't say I like it as much as you do, in spite of the lovely wooded hills. Like you, I'm glad they're too steep to build on and I'd love to see the trees in their autumn colours. But the hills crowd in on the town too much. There isn't enough flat land for a proper town at all. The river and canal are very nice but the road and the railway have to squeeze through the valley too. There's too much traffic and too much noise!

You'll have to come and see me in Newley. Then you can find fault with *my* home town!

Best wishes,
Mary

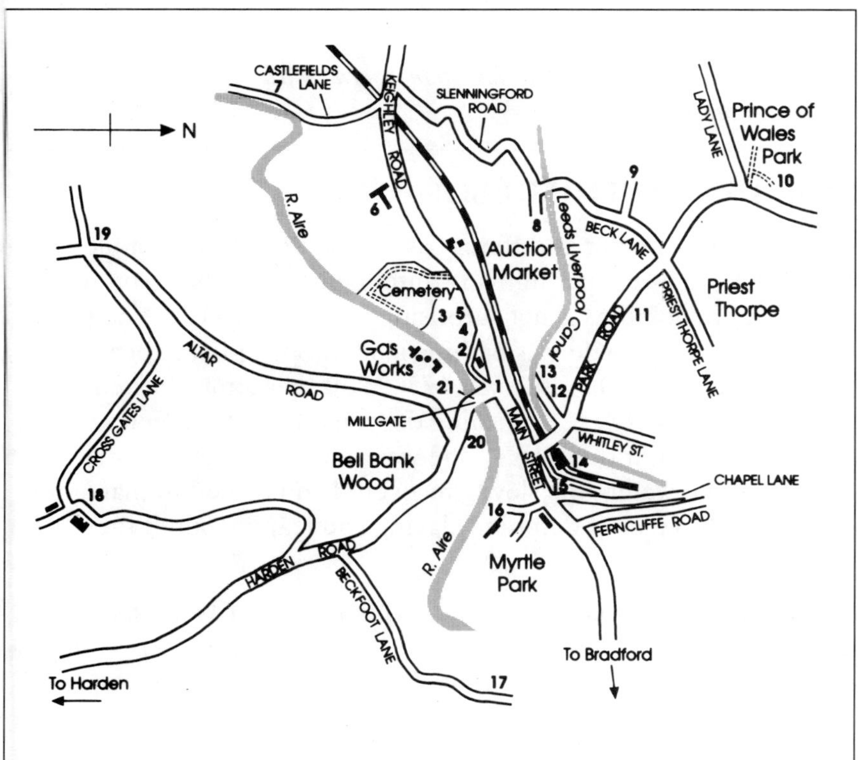

KEY TO MAP

1 Old Main Street
2 Parish Church
3 Bailey Hills
4 Schoolmaster's House
5 Weavers' Cottages
6 The Grammar School
7 Castlefield Mill
8 Five Rise Locks
9 Gawthorpe Hall
10 Market Cross & Stocks
11 Monk Barn
12 National School
13 Lime Street
14 The Railway
15 Mechanics' Institute
16 Myrtle Grove
17 Beckfoot Bridge & Farm
18 St Ives
19 Druid's Altar
20 Brown Cow Inn
21 Ireland Bridge

SECTION B

Choose **one** *of the following writing tasks. Your answer should follow* **exactly** *the instructions given. You are advised to write approximately 250 words.*

1 You run a language school and offer tuition in English for a certain examination, such as the Certificate in Advanced English. Write for your brochure or booklet a description of the new examination and the sort of people who would benefit from studying for it. If you wish you can add some comments about the sort of tuition your school can offer.

2 A man has written to a health column because he is worried by a recurrent dream that people are laughing at him because he is getting shorter and shorter. He wants to know whether the dream reveals any secrets about his personality. Pretend that you are a doctor or a psychiatrist and write an answer for publication.

3 You run a shop and find that you cannot afford to pay one of your suppliers on time. Write to the company concerned explaining your problem, its cause and how they can help you. You can make up any details that would help to make your answer more realistic.

4 Write instructions to help a blind person to use a certain piece of equipment which you are accustomed to using, such as a certain type of music centre. (Your instructions will be turned into braille – a sort of lettering that is 'read' by touch.)

PAPER 3 ENGLISH IN USE 1 hour 30 minutes

SECTION A

1 *Read the article below and for questions* **1–16** *circle the letter next to the word which best fits each space. The first answer has been given as an example.*

DOLPHIN TO THE RESCUE

People often claim that humans and animals are not as different as they appear. For example, dolphins are often **(1)** . . . with human – or even super-human – intelligence and also a sort of **(2)** . . . with human beings. This **(3)** . . . to dolphins is not surprising in view of **(4)** . . . like the **(5)** . . . one, which happened in 1983. A lawyer's wife was bathing alone from a private beach in Florida. She had only just **(6)** . . . into the water when she was **(7)** . . . off by a strong current. She swallowed water and was beginning to lose **(8)** . . . , wishing desperately that someone would come and rescue her. And she tells how at this **(9)** . . . she was given 'a tremendous shove' and found herself **(10)** . . . out of the water. She slowly recovered and turned to thank her **(11)** . . . . But there was no one about, only a pair of dolphins playing and leaping out of the water a few metres offshore.

At this point a man came running up to **(12)** . . . that he had seen what he had **(13)** . . . for a dead body being pushed ashore by one of the dolphins. Now this is not an obscure **(14)** . . . of an incident which happened in the dim and **(15)** . . . past. It happened in our own times and was witnessed by a number of **(16)** . . . .

1	(A) credited	B awarded	C attributed	D reckoned
2	A likeness	B attraction	C sympathy	D fellowship
3	A regard	B viewpoint	C attitude	D aspect
4	A occasions	B incidents	C scenes	D circumstances
5	A next	B following	C subsequent	D below
6	A swum	B emerged	C entered	D gone
7	A taken	B carried	C fetched	D transported
8	A sight	B life	C awareness	D consciousness
9	A instance	B time	C moment	D occasion
10	A staggering	B hauling	C rescuing	D appearing
11	A saver	B companion	C rescuer	D assistant
12	A speak	B tell	C say	D shout
13	A taken	B supposed	C recognised	D supposed
14	A narrative	B account	C tale	D version
15	A unreliable	B historical	C ancient	D distant
16	A onlookers	B watchers	C viewers	D spectators

2 *Complete the following report by writing the missing words in the spaces provided. Use* ***only one word*** *in each space.*

A NEGLECTED REPAIR

Mrs Dawson is a widow of 78, living alone in a terraced house in Richmond Hill, built a century ago and belonging to the local City Council.

In August 1985 she reported **(1)** __________ the local housing manager **(2)** __________ the down-pipe from the front guttering was cracked. The repair **(3)** __________ not done and dampness spread **(4)** __________ the house. This created other problems: wallpaper **(5)** __________ to peel off the walls, and fungus developed. Mrs Dawson's carpets and curtains began to **(6)** __________ wet. Her gas fires were insufficient to keep the damp at bay.

Finally, **(7)** __________ several complaints, the fractured down-pipe was replaced – this February. Unfortunately, the house remained damp **(8)** __________ the weather grew warmer, and problems then arose from the plaster as it dried **(9)** __________, and also from the window and door frames.

As **(10)** __________ happens, Mrs Dawson is a sprightly lady **(11)** __________ is coping well with a problem which **(12)** __________ have been solved promptly **(13)** __________ a cost of £10. But the delay has created a health risk, deterioration of the property **(14)** __________ will involve greater expense, and an unnecessary pressure on a vulnerable **(15)** __________ of the community.

SECTION B

3 *In most lines of the following text there is* **one** *unnecessary word. It is either grammatically incorrect or it does not suit the sense of the text.*

Read the text, put a line through each unnecessary word and then write the word in the space provided at the end of the line. Some lines are correct. Indicate these lines with a tick (✔) against the line number. The first two lines have been done as examples.

THE RACE FOR SURVIVAL

Imagine the Earth without any life. The higher ground would	1	✔
be mostly bare ~~of~~ rock and ice. There would be storms as	2	of
we experience them now. Winds would blow, no rain would fall,	3	
and rivers would flow along courses like to their present	4	
ones. The world would have a nightmarish similarity to the	5	
present Earth. There would be Africa and Asia, the Europe	6	
and the Americas but all them would lie inert and bare.	7	
Let us suppose that all the life which actually exists	8	
on the Earth were suddenly to die. If such a thing was happened	9	
the oxygen in the atmosphere would break the dead material	10	
down and cause it to disappear away in a month or so.	11	
Oxygen even attacks things that are well alive. Thus life	12	
as we know it is in a race between regenerating itself and	13	
in being burned up, a race that is balanced on a razor's	14	
edge and depends crucially on rainfall. Where there is plenty	15	
of rain the life wins. But where there is only a little	16	
of rain the burning process turns the landscape into desert.	17	

4 *Look at the diagram and read the explanation, which is in formal English. On page 36 a lecturer has changed the wording to suit his audience. Complete the passage by writing the missing words in the spaces on the right.*

Use **one word** *in each space.*

The diagram shows some of the buildings at a boarding school in this locality. The buildings are the pupils' living and sleeping accommodation. The larger boxes in the diagram represent the bedrooms, which are situated on the first floor; these boxes are subdivided into squares, each of which represents a bed.

Many of the pupils recently succumbed to colds, and the numbers show the order in which they reported sick.

The evidence is inconclusive, but in Professor Hoyle's opinion the germs descended through the atmosphere unevenly, so that different numbers reached the ground in different places. The initial effects were felt at Hazelwood and Taylor Houses, where the majority of the pupils caught colds.

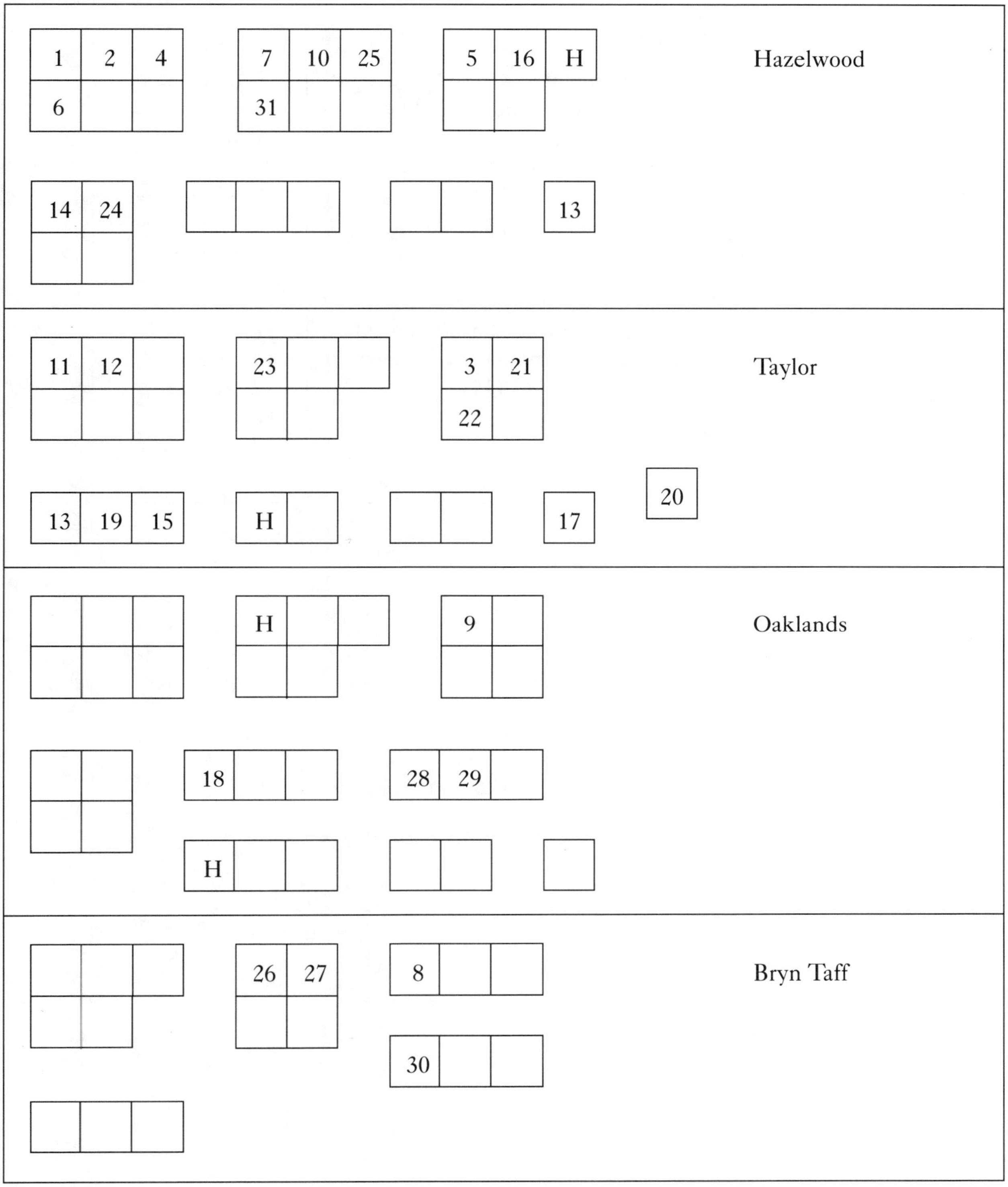

Schematic plan of dormitories at Howell's for four houses: Hazelwood, Taylor, Oaklands and Bryn Taff. Boxes represent rooms, compartments within boxes are occupied beds. Numbers show order of victims reporting to the school nurse. H stands for a week-day boarder who had influenza over the weekend.

DOWN COME THE GERMS!

The diagram shows some of the buildings at a local (1) . . . school. The pupils (2) . . . and (3) . . . in the buildings. The larger boxes in the diagram (4) . . . for the bedrooms, which (5) . . . on the first floor; these boxes are (6) . . . up into squares – (7) . . . for each bed. Many of the pupils recently (8) . . . colds, and the numbers show the order in which they (9) . . . ill. The evidence does not (10) . . . anything, but Fred Hoyle (11) . . . that the germs (12) . . . down through the air unevenly. The number landing in different places was not the (13) . . . . Hazelwood and Taylor Houses were affected (14) . . . and (15) . . . of the pupils caught colds.	1 __________ 2 __________ 3 __________ 4 __________ 5 __________ 6 __________ 7 __________ 8 __________ 9 __________ 10 __________ 11 __________ 12 __________ 13 __________ 14 __________ 15 __________

SECTION C

5 *Choose the best phrase or sentence (given below the text) to fill each of the blanks in the following text. Write one letter (A – G) in each of the numbered spaces. Two of the suggested answers do not fit at all.*

GOOD AND BAD TRAVELLERS

People fall into two distinct types – good travellers and bad ones. Good travellers know where they want to go, prepare efficiently, and reach their destination without any serious misadventure, delay or complication. **(1)** __________ It is rather uncanny and indefinable – a sort of good fortune that follows good travellers on their way and sees them through to their destination. Somehow it wards off the troubles that beset their 'bad traveller' brothers. The distinction between these classes of traveller shows up most clearly on railway journeys. True enough, good travellers can be faced with broken down, re-routed or even cancelled trains. But it seems to happen less often to them. And the consequences are far less disastrous.

(2) __________ He knows the alternative routes and finds an alternative train at the instant he wants it. Believe it or not, I have known a good traveller to reach his destination early simply because he jumped on the right alternative train and circumvented the cause of everyone else's delay!

Now let us think about the born bad traveller. We can spend more time on him because there is more to say. Also – let's face it – his antics are far more entertaining. The bad traveller typically starts his day with alarm clock problems. **(3)** __________ (The chances are that he set it wrongly the night before.) Now picture him rushing round in a panic. He dresses, shaves and eats his breakfast almost simultaneously. This is something of a virtuoso performance, but any impartial observer knows that it bodes very ill for the traveller's prospects! Suspicions are confirmed when his taxi arrives – amazingly he remembered to book one the night before – and whisks him off to his local station – without that vital briefcase of his. Away goes the taxi just as he realises his mistake. There is nothing for it but to wait for another taxi to take him home to collect it.

At last he is back at the station. He hears his train coming and by sprinting across the footbridge he manages to miss it by the narrowest margin. All he wants is a local train to connect with his main-line train to the city. He thinks of using a taxi, but he knows the next train should make it – with maybe two or three minutes to spare. **(4)** __________ Perhaps the bad traveller's presence has somehow caused the breakdown. It may just be that other passengers – or indeed the railway company – should seek to debar him from their trains. This raises questions of human rights which are best debated some other time. For the moment let us just picture our traveller. While mechanics tinker in the driver's cab he watches forlornly from the window as his intended train glides from the station and gathers speed. He stares with envious eyes at the comfortably-seated passengers. He envies not only their comfort but also their 'good traveller' status. **(5)** __________ At the moment there is one inescapable fact tormenting his brain – that the other train has two empty seats which he has booked, one for himself and one for his briefcase. Ah yes, there they go – gliding emptily past in coach H.

When his crippled train finally reaches the platform he cannot obtain information about any later trains. Then he sees one – a train which is just about to depart. He leaps aboard and the train sets off – in the wrong direction. Too late, he goes down the corridor to ask for advice . . .

A A good traveller faced with a cancelled train knows what to do.

B This is partly a matter of competence, but something else is involved as well.

C It goes off late and needless to say he is quick to blame the mechanism.

D Or, to put it another way, it is easy to tell what sort of traveller this person is.

E There are usually plenty of taxis but because he has 'bad travellers' luck', there are very few running this particular morning.

F This is something that a bad traveller senses intuitively, though he may not have consciously turned it over in his mind.

G However, it is doomed to break down just within sight of its destination.

6 *A friend has written to ask whether you think he/she would enjoy a visit to London. Before writing your reply you make some notes.*

You must use all the words in the **same order** *as the notes. You may add words and change the form of words where necessary. Look carefully at the example which has been done for you.*

a Only been London once but great time.

b By train – quick, comfortable.

c Some good museums Kensington area – liked very much.

d Museums interest you/bore you?

e After museums found cheap hotel – only afford stay single night.

f Student like you, so careful with money!

g Evening meal in room, bed early.

h Next morning post office so send postcards.

i Spent pm sightseeing, evening by bus to station train home.

Dear Jane

Thanks for your letter. You asked me what I thought of London and whether I'd recommend you to go.

a *I've only been to London once but I had a great time.*

b ______________________________

c ______________________________

d ______________________________

e ______________________________

f ______________________________

g ______________________________

h ______________________________

i ______________________________

So there you are. It was very tiring, but, yes, I think you should go if you can. It costs a lot but you'll have a good time!

Best wishes,

TEST TWO

PAPER 4 LISTENING 35 minutes

SECTION A

You will hear someone describing the view from a balcony in a city centre. As you listen complete sentences ***1–12****. You will hear the piece twice.*

In referring to Salt's Mill the speaker mentions **1** [ ]

beyond and the surrounding **2** [ ].

She is surprised that the lights are on at the football ground because

3 [ ].

She goes on to mention the airport, which can be picked out because

4 [ ].

She says that many people think the Cathedral is **5** [ ]

but she mentions the **6** [ ] which people can always enjoy

there at lunchtimes.

If people look slightly to the right they should be able to see the mosque and also the

7 [ ] and the **8** [ ].

However, they may have difficulty in seeing properly because

9 [ ].

She says that the city is unusual in building new **10** [ ].

As well as having conservatories on the balconies they

have **11** [ ] on the

12 [ ].

SECTION B

You will hear two people discussing the changes that have been made to a house. For **questions 13–23** *fill in the blamk spaces in the table.*

Listen carefully as you will hear the piece **ONLY ONCE**.

How the area was used before		How the area is used now	
13			Conservatory
14			Kitchen
15			Dining room
	Garden	16	
	Smallest bedroom	17	
	Largest bedroom	18	
	Garage	19	
20			Porch
	Pantry and washroom	21	
	Tool shed	22	
	Children's playroom	23	

SECTION C

You will hear a series of questions and answers to do with money. For **Questions 24–35**, *complete the notes using a few words; you do* **not** *need to write full sentences. You will hear the piece* ***twice.***

The speaker invites people to ask questions because he knows that

24	.

He says the musician should make it clear that he | 25 | |

with his instruments and is a | 26 | | musician.

The lady with the white hair is a | 27 | . |

The speaker tells her that Premium bonds are for | 28 | |

people. In his opinion she should cash her Bonds and use some of the

money to | 29 | . |

The plumber asks whether he should | 30 | |

but the speaker says he should use | 31 | . |

The boy has | 32 | | weeks in which to save up his money for

Christmas, and the speaker assumes that he is going to | 33 | |

with it.

The last person who asks a question keeps her money | 34 | . |

The speaker thinks that she would be asking for trouble if

35	.

SECTION D

Now look at section D for the last part of the test. You will hear various people describing their problems.

TASK ONE lists the problems. Put them in the order in which you hear them by writing a number from 1–5 in each box. Three boxes will remain empty.

TASK 1

Missing relative	36	
Lost property	37	
Missed train	38	
Back pain	39	
Road accident	40	
Damaged clothing	41	
Faulty television	42	
Trouble in getting library books	43	

TASK TWO lists the places where the people are. Put the places in the order in which they occur by writing a number from 1–5 in each box. Three boxes will remain empty.

You will hear the series twice.

TASK 2

Garage or service station	44	
Library	45	
Railway station	46	
Doctor's surgery	47	
Home	48	
Street	49	
Inside a shop	50	
Police station	51	

TEST TWO

PAPER 5 SPEAKING 15 minutes

QUESTION 1 *(candidate 1)*

The examiner will ask you to describe the photograph on page 89 to your partner, who has a photograph which is related to yours in some way.

At the end of one minute the examiner will ask your partner to say what the relationship between your pictures is. You should then try to reach agreement with your partner.

NB: The instructions would not appear on the examination material in the real exam. They would be conveyed orally by the examiner.

QUESTION 1 *(candidate 2)*

The examiner will ask your partner to describe a photograph to you. The photograph on page 93 is related to your partner's in some way.

After one minute you may ask short questions if you wish or find it necessary. The examiner will then ask you to say what the relationship between the photographs is. You should then try to reach agreement with your partner.

QUESTION 2 *(candidate 1)*

The examiner will ask your partner to describe one of the six photographs below to you.

At the end of one minute the examiner will ask you to say which photograph your partner was describing.

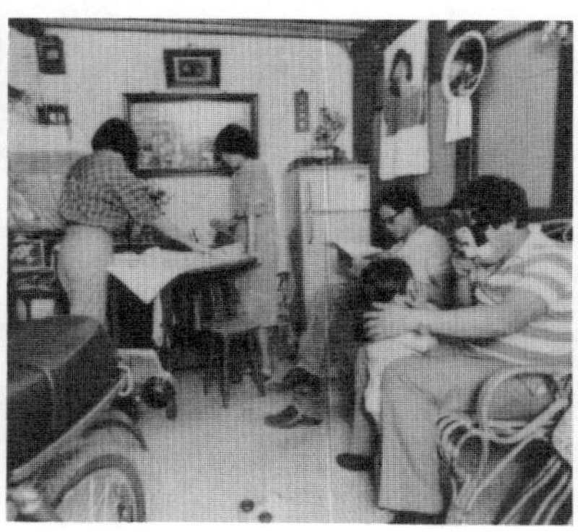

QUESTION 2 *(candidate 2)*

The examiner will ask you to describe one of the six photographs below to your partner (who has the same six photographs).

At the end of one minute the examiner will ask your partner to say which photograph you were describing.

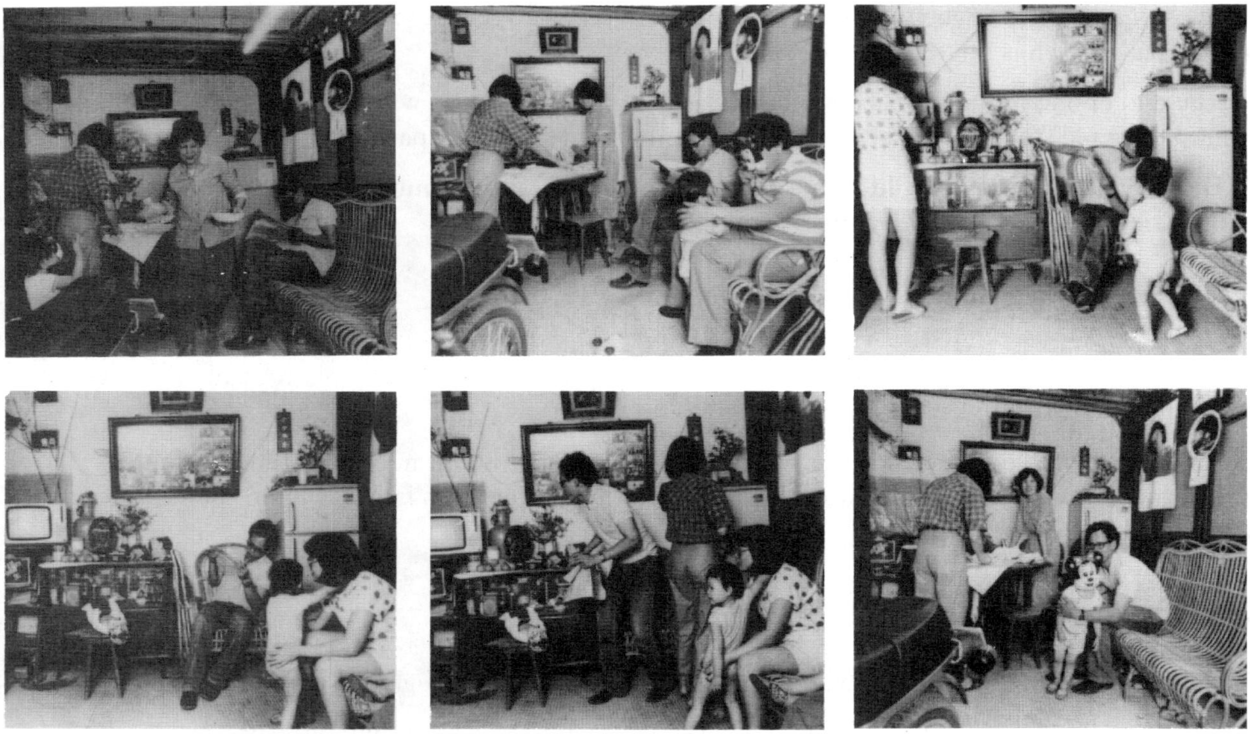

QUESTION 3 *(both candidates)*

Look at the photographs, which come from a toy catalogue.

Discuss with your partner what they say about how people bring their children up. You must either reach agreement or 'agree to disagree'. Make sure that you understand your partner's opinion. At the end of three minutes you will be asked to report your decision to the examiners, and take part in further discussions.

TEST THREE

PAPER 1 READING 1 hour

FIRST TEXT QUESTIONS 1–7

These questions are based on a light-hearted article about modern libraries.

For questions 1–7 you must choose which of the extracts **A–G** *on the following page match the numbered gaps in the text. There is one additional extract which does not belong in any of the gaps. Indicate your answers* ***on the separate answer sheet.***

Hooked on Books

Many people think that libraries are dreary places where everyone has to creep round in a solemn, almost ashamed sort of silence. But those who hold such views have probably not been inside a library for years – or even decades. Nowadays, libraries are brighter, far more inviting places than ever before. Sometimes you could even call them lively, verging perhaps on the vulgar and rowdy.

1	

There may be 'no talking' notices; and the books are normally 'reference only', which means that if one takes your fancy you'll have to stay in the reference department and read it there. But let's face facts: here among these dusty tomes there are very few books that you'll want to read for pleasure, relaxation or to escape from life's troubles.

2	

In place of the all-pervasive silence you're likely to find young children scurrying, chattering and even playing hide and seek round the walls of books; old folk, too, are likely to be enjoying themselves – completely at ease as they gossip or simply lounge in the chairs.

3	

I'm not quite sure why this is so; they can't be worried about litter; there's plenty of that on the floor and no one bothers to clear it up. Perhaps books still matter just a little and it's thought undesirable to get the pages glued together with chewing gum or a sticky sweet. Or perhaps they want you to patronise the library cafe. One day I'll ask the reason for the strange prohibition on eating and drinking.

4	

Maybe you'd like a happy medium – something between the austere prohibitions of libraries past and the permissiveness of libraries today. But if you're set on finding a particular book – perhaps a novel or an old-style romance – you can probably manage to cope with the noise and the hurly-burly.

5	

Gone are the days of leafing through a set of cards and risking the calamity I had as a child of spilling the lot all over the floor. Nowadays – barring fused electrics – the information you want will leap to the screen at the touch of one or two buttons. There they are – directions to that book you've been meaning to read for years. So off you go, picking your way among sprawling legs and finally reaching the appropriate shelf – only to find that the book you require is stolen, lost or out on loan.

6	

They've been stealing, losing and borrowing books for donkey's years. And yes, they've been neglecting them too – scribbling in them and using the leaves of choice editions as cigarette papers.

7	

There are far, far more facilities than I've time to mention. What about the 'sound and vision' department, where you can borrow records and videos? What about the archive where you can investigate your family history? And don't forget the lunchtime concerts at many public libraries? These are just examples, so go again – and again and again.

A Libraries have so much to offer and you've only yourself to blame if you've not been using your local library service to the full.

B Most libraries do have a reference department for serious study, and here, if anywhere, you can still find a little of the old, rather staid formality.

C You may perhaps feel that there's too much noise, especially if decades have passed since you last went book-hunting.

D These days your search for a given book will be aided or hindered – depending on your keyboard skills – by the presence of a computerised index.

E If a librarian intervenes she will do so to stop someone smoking or eating – still regarded as serious offences.

F Don't be too upset. On reflection, you'll probably agree that the library's regular users deserve priority.

G Of course, playing loud music would be going too far in any department of any library.

H For recreational books you'll need to go to the lending department or 'popular library'. And here you'll find just how enormously libraries have changed.

SECOND TEXT QUESTIONS 8–18

Answer the following questions by referring to the extract on page 47.

These questions ask you to choose the correct title for each paragraph (1–6). ***A–I*** *list the possible titles.* ***On your answer sheet****, indicate your answer to each question by choosing from the list* ***A–I****.*

Note: *There is only* ***one*** *answer to each question..*

8	Paragraph 1	A	Efficiency first
9	Paragraph 2	B	Ford at his Best
10	Paragraph 3	C	The five Dollar Day
11	Paragraph 4	D	Hanging onto Power
12	Paragraph 5	E	Ford's Two Faces
13	Paragraph 6	F	Sacked Workers' Anger
		G	The Company Under Edsel Ford
		H	Unrest and Bitterness
		I	A New Line in Cars

The Two Henry Fords

1) The public knows two Henry Fords. There is the kindly, benign Ford, a man of rough manners, down-to-earth humour and sound common-sense: an ordinary man made extraordinary by hard work and perseverance and his own mechanical and organizational genius. He was eccentric, of course – he detested cigarettes and allowed no one to smoke in his factories. He pronounced on public issues with the confidence of ignorance. He even, it is rumoured, set his sights on the Presidency of the United States, although he was in fact practically illiterate. He once described the word 'commenced' as a technical term, and claimed he seldom read books since 'they mess up my mind'. His cars brought untold benefits to untold numbers. His starting of the 'Five Dollar Day' in 1914 made him a great benefactor of the working classes, while the establishment of the Ford Foundation in 1936 made him rank among the world's greatest philanthropists.

2) But there was the other Ford: the man who sacrificed partners, colleagues, workers, even family, to his god of mass production. There is a German word *Fordismus* which conjures up the epitome of maximum industrial productivity, where everything yields place to the tyranny of economic efficiency. The Five Dollar Day and the conveyor belt meant more money for the workers. It also meant insecurity, for skilled labour could be dispensed with, and the lure of high wages meant an assured pool of willing labour ready to step into the shoes of any dissatisfied or incompetent worker. Indeed, on the very day that the Five dollar wage was announced, violence flared at Ford's factory as men clamoured for work. Ford was also a bigot, who allowed his personal prejudices to govern his actions and his dealings with men.

3) How can we account for these contradictions? It is partly a question of time, for until the middle of the 1920s Henry Ford was a national folk hero, whose enterprise symbolised the American dream of earthly rewards for the ordinary self-made man. But as Ford grew older, his natural authoritarian views were fostered and made dangerous by his wealth. His words were power, and the yes-men around him did as their master wanted.

4) The personality of Henry Ford continued to dominate the Ford company as he stumbled towards senility. He became increasingly suspicious of his subordinates, and allowed his only son Edsel (who had been nominal president of the company since 1918) little independence. Ford's weaknesses lay in the organization of his company, if 'organization' it can be called. He distrusted 'experts' and he avoided as far as possible specialized executive positions. In theory, any job was open to anyone, yet no job was safe, and many of Ford's leading executives were sacked. William Knudsen, who eventually became president of General Motors, left in 1921, during Ford's highly characteristic reaction to a catastrophic slump. This was to purge the organization (the office staff was cut by half), cut costs in every way, produce more at lower prices, and force thousands of cars upon the desperate dealers.

5) In the mid-1920s Ford's adherence to a single, very basic car became a liability, as the American public began to look for something more stylish and less obviously mass-produced. Moreover, the very reliability of the Model T's posed formidable competition, as millions of second-hand Model T's came on the market. In May 1927, with sales slipping alarmingly, Henry Ford, now an old man of sixty-four, made another momentous decision. The Model T would be scrapped and the whole plant closed for nearly a year while experiments and machinery for a new car, the 'Model A' , were undertaken. For a time the new car was very successful, but Ford's pre-eminence was gone for ever. When depression struck in 1929, sales of the Model A fell away.

6) Henry Ford, once the workers' champion with his Five Dollar Day, the man who considered himself an ordinary workman and hated the capitalists, became himself a byword for exploitation. Not unnaturally, therefore, among the scores of protest and hunger marches which occurred in the USA in the midst of the great depression, was one by unemployed people, aimed at Ford's plant. A procession of several hundred took place in the spring of 1932. Gunfire started, some from Ford's own company police (Ford actually had more police on his payroll than the whole of Detroit City). Four of the marchers were killed, and twenty were wounded. The tragedy served to confirm Ford's evil reputation among workers. When Edsel Ford died in 1943, Henry became company president once more. Senility now added to the dangers of his personality. Not until 1945, at the age of eighty-two, did he finally yield power, and it was left to his grandson Henry Ford II to revitalise the most famous automobile company in the world.

QUESTIONS 14–18

For questions 14–18 you must choose the answer which you think best completes each unfinished statement about the text. ***On your answer sheet****, indicate the letter* **A**, **B**, **C** *and* **D** *against the number of each question. Give* ***one answer only*** *to each question.*

14 Ford had a mixed reputation because

A he changed with the times.
B his faults became more pronounced as he aged.
C he was eccentric and ignorant.
D skilled workers knew he could do without them.

15 Until the mid 1920s Ford was a national hero because

A he had got on in life by his own efforts.
B he introduced the Five Dollar Day.
C he was the workers' champion.
D he was powerful and people did as he wanted.

16 In his younger days what mattered most to Ford was

A becoming President.
B efficient production methods.
C looking after his workers well.
D being obeyed by the people around him.

17 Ford did not mind sacking ordinary workers because

A there were plenty of other men who wanted jobs.
B he did not need their skills.
C he wanted to make cars cheaply and efficiently.
D he had a suspicious and distrustful nature.

18 In the 1920s Ford

A sold second-hand Model T cars.
B took advantage of dealers who were desperate for his cars.
C stuck to making Model Ts for too long.
D began to give Edsel Ford a little independence.

THIRD TEXT QUESTIONS 19–35

Answer these questions by filling in the table on your answer sheet using the information contained in the reading passages, which deal with things we might want to take when travelling. Indicate your answer to each question by choosing from the list A–N. Some of the choices may be required more than once.

Note: *where more than one piece of information is needed you may give the answers* **in any order**.

A	Quick at 110V
B	Hot after use
C	Lid comes off
D	Can't get badly overheated
E	Risk from long flex
F	• extra flex
G	'Minimum' marker
H	Folding handle
I	Cool blow feature
J	Element needs covering
K	Carrying pouch
L	No carrying pouch
M	Two settings
N	Flex around 180cm long

Product	Safety Advice and Information	Features Found in Several Models	Good or Bad Features of Particular Models	
			Model	Feature
Kettles	19			
	20			
	21	22	En Voyage	23 ....
Elements in Cups	24			
Irons	25	26		
		27		
Hairdryers		28	Morphy Richards	32 ....
		29	Lloytron	33 ....
		30	BaByliss	34 ....
		31		35 ....

Getting into Hot Water

When considering a kettle to carry around with you, it's worth thinking about how much water you'll be boiling: is the cuppa just for yourself or will it be tea for two?

The maximum capacity for the seven kettles we tested ranged from a third of a litre (enough for two cups of tea) to nearly three-quarters of a litre, or enough for about four cups. If you want to boil only a small amount of water, always make sure that you cover the element: some of the kettles we looked at didn't have a 'minimum fill' line. We also tested a water heater which is like a kettle element with a handle, which you put into the cup to heat the water.

SMALL BUT SLOW Although the kettles we tested hold less water than a full-sized one, they can take longer to boil. To see how well the kettle performed, we boiled the maximum volume they could hold. All the kettles took less than nine minutes to boil at 240V (taking up to five times as long at 110V). The exception was the En Voyage kettle which was only slightly slower to boil at the lower voltage.

SAFETY MATTERS All the kettles and water heaters passed our electrical safety tests. But because you'll be using the kettle in a strange environment, possibly on a bedside table, you should be particularly careful about safety, especially if there are small children around. None of the kettles we tested had locking or even hinged lids which can help to reduce the water spillage if the kettle's knocked over. And although you'll need a flex which can reach sockets conveniently, you need to be careful not to let it overhang where the kettle might be pulled off.

You'll need to be particularly careful with water heaters because they can stay hot for some time after being switched off. So put them somewhere safe while they're cooling down.

A Pressing Time

You've unpacked, had a cup of tea made with your travel kettle, and are about to go for dinner, when you notice your clothes are a bit crumpled. Help is at hand in the form of travel irons and steam brushes. But don't expect your travel iron to match the performance of the one you left at home. A lot of members who used travel irons said they took longer to do the ironing, were less powerful, too light, and couldn't remove stubborn creases.

We've tested four steam travel irons and two dry irons, all of which were about a third lighter than a full-sized iron – a major consideration when you're lugging your luggage.

IRONING OUT PROBLEMS Packing your travel iron will be less of a problem if you look for one with a folding or detachable handle. And once you've got to your destination, remember that you won't have an ironing board so you'll need to put a towel or blanket underneath anything you iron. Make sure the iron has a long enough flex, since you may have to use it some distance from the socket. The flexes on the irons we tested were all around 180cm.

SAFETY MATTERS All the irons we tested were dual voltage, which means they can be used at both 220/240V and 110/120V.

All the irons were fitted with non-resetting thermal cut-outs, so if the iron overheated it would automatically switch itself off and all passed our electrical safety tests. But once cut out, the iron couldn't be used again until the thermal cut-out had been replaced.

Hairdriers

If you already own a compact hairdrier, you may find that there's not much difference between the travel driers we've tested and the one you've already got – but if you go further afield than Europe – to the States, for example – you may find that your normal hairdrier won't work at the lower voltage. If you're looking for something light and compact to take on your travels, we've tested seven travel hairdriers all of which have two settings: low speed, low heat, and high speed, high heat. The Babyliss 815 also had a cool-air button for setting curls. They were all electrically safe.

All the hairdriers except the Lloytron and Morphy Richards had a carrying pouch. The Morphy Richards HD761 only operated at 240V, so it wouldn't be advisable to use it in countries with a 110/120V electricity supply.

A DRYING TIME Look at the length of the flex when choosing a hairdrier, since sockets may not always be next to a mirror – and don't ever take the hairdrier into the bathroom if this is the only mirror available. All the hairdriers we looked at have flex lengths of around 180cm, except the BaByliss which is 235cm. To find out how well the travel driers dried hair, we asked a group of people to try them out for a week. All were considered to take an acceptable time to dry hair, but only the Lloytron Traveller, Philips Voyager, and Russell Hobbs Travel Line were picked out as acceptable travel hairdriers since they're light, compact and easy to use.

Hairdriers are awkwardly shaped items, so it's useful if they've got a folding handle. If you want to take styling attachments, even though they're not very heavy they may add to the bulk of your suitcase.

FOURTH TEXT QUESTIONS 36-40

Read the following extract and answer questions 36–40.

Pointers To Learning

1) A lecture may seem to be well organised in the lecturer's notes but have no apparent pattern when delivered. Ideally students should be able to state the intended organisation, and how one fact is broadly related to the rest, at any time during the lecture, firstly because they need to take notes if the amount of information to be retained exceeds the amount they can remember, and secondly because these links are essential to understanding.

2) It follows, of course, that a lecture is likely to be more effective if its organisation is given at the beginning. This can usually be done very naturally as an explanation of how the lecturer's objectives are to be achieved. Certainly the dictum "first tell 'em what you're going to tell 'em. Then tell 'em what you've told 'em," can usefully be applied to lectures and is particularly appropriate to those who teach a difficult subject or who cannot easily get down to the students' level of understanding.

3) Some lecturers may feel that by summarising all they intend to say at the beginning, they will have 'shot their bolt' and have nothing left with which to arouse interest when attention flags. In this case the summary needs to be given in a way that whets the appetite and the elaboration of points will require interesting details, visual illustration, humour and an occasional anecdote.

4) Itemising points has several advantages. First, each item provides a peg on which detail may be hung. Secondly, while it may be obvious to the lecturer that he is going on to a fresh point this is not so obvious to the listener, least of all the student who is not already familiar with the topic. Thirdly, if a student day-dreams, or has microsleeps, he may easily lose the thread of an argument. If points are itemised he will know when he misses one and he will be able to pick up the lecturer's drift again more easily, latching on to the point that follows. He may also be able to fill in the missing point with the help of another student later. Just as most people are unaware that they dream 3 or 4 times each night so most students are probably unaware how much their minds wander during lectures. Fourthly, itemisation is an aid to memory. Revision from notes is more thorough if the student knows "there are five points to be remembered on this topic and seven on the other."

5) The organisation of a lecture will be clearer if the points are written on the board immediately after being mentioned. Lecturers who are not confident of their ability on the blackboard are tempted to neglect it. One way over this difficulty is to use an overhead projector which may show either normal handwriting done at the time, or prepared acetate sheets which may be progressively displayed as the lecture develops. Alternatively, a handout containing the main headings well spaced, with blanks in between for the students to add supplementary detail, is useful; and since handouts may be passed on to absentees, they are particularly valuable at the beginning of a course or at other times when it is important to convey the organisation of subject matter. Such displays of lecture organisation (using the blackboard, overhead projector, handouts, or possibly other methods such as flannel graphs and charts) play a particularly important part in aiding comprehension when a flow diagram or other complex form is used because the relations between possibly abstract ideas can be pointed out visually.

In brief, we can say that information must be organised in the *students*' mind and not just in the lecturer's.

For questions ***36–40*** *say which of the notes below* ***(A–H)*** *best sums up each of the first five paragraphs. Indicate your answers* ***on the separate answer sheet.***

Note: *There is only* ***one*** *answer to each question.*

36	paragraph 1	**A**	Put it up on the blackboard!
37	paragraph 2	**B**	Ways of making key points clear.
38	paragraph 3	**C**	Maintaining interest.
39	paragraph 4	**D**	Clear structures important.
40	paragraph 5	**E**	Wandering minds.
		F	State structure at start.
		G	Why 'key points' are useful.
		H	filling in the detail.

FOURTH TEXT QUESTIONS 41–45

For questions ***41–45*** *you must choose the answer which you think best completes the unfinished statements about the text.* ***On your answer sheet*** *indicate the letter* ***A, B, C*** *or* ***D*** *against the number of each question. Give* ***one answer only*** *to each question.*

41 A clear idea of what a lecture is all about is important because

A students must always finish up with well-organised notes.
B it can capture the students' interest.
C it can help the lecturer to present things more clearly.
D students must see how a topic hangs together if they are to understand it.

42 Students are likely to take in a lecture better if the lecturer

A gives them a summary before he begins.
B arranges what he has to say in the best possible way.
C improves his blackboard technique.
D gives out or displays comprehensive notes.

43 Some lecturers do not like giving an outline of their lectures at the start because

A their notes are well-planned but they cannot make things clear to their students.
B they do not like repeating themselves.
C they are afraid that the rest of the lecture will seem like an anti-climax.
D they lack confidence in using the blackboard.

44 Students whose minds wander easily

A may fail to make sense of points in a lecture.
B lose arguments because they cannot follow what is being said.
C have an ability to 'tune in' easily when their attention returns.
D depend on other students to help them follow the lecture.

45 Lecturers can use an overhead projector

A to present key points in advance.
B to present key points as they arise.
C to help students understand what a 'flow diagram' is.
D to show students normal handwriting done on the spot.

PAPER 2 WRITING 2 hours

SECTION A

Your friend has written from the United States asking you to check on holiday accommodation for him. After reading his letter (below) you do as he asks and go to the tourist office, where you see the advertisements shown.

Write the sort of reply your friend wants. You can add any necessary extra details to make your answer more complete, but make sure you **do not change** *the information given.*

You are advised to write approximately 250 words.

Porta's Box
Central Avenue West
Miami, Florida, USA

18th June 1991

Dear John

Do you think you could help us?

The three of us are coming to England for a fortnight's holiday at the end of next month. We want to stay in Cromer and it's too late to write to the tourist office, as they probably won't reply by airmail. As you live on the spot, do you think you could go to the office for me and ask what accommodation there is? If you can recommend one or two suitable houses or flats - and tell us of any we need to avoid - I can ring them long-distance and see about booking.
I think you know our basic requirements - privacy, one or two outdoor activities - in spite of my arthritic leg - and lots of home comforts. By the way - I can stifle my smoking urge if I really have to; they probably ban cigarettes in some of the better places.
We can afford £100 a week or a little more. We're not quite broke, in spite of an extra mouth to feed!

Best wishes,

Tony, Mary and Caroline.

Please write soon!

SYMBOLS

Information about facilities has been provided in this guide by means of symbols, as shown in the key below. If you want somewhere with say a four poster bed or a swimming pool, then look for the appropriate symbol.

- Children welcome (a number following gives minimum age).
- Not all bedrooms have hot and cold water.
- M Payment for bedroom heating by coin meter.
- Ground floor bedrooms.
- R Radio in all bedrooms.
- Television in all bedrooms.
- Tea/coffee making facilities in all bedrooms.
- UL Unlicensed (alcholic drinks not served).
- Packed lunch provided on request.
- Lounge for residents' use.
- TV Television available.
- Night porter on duty.
- Passenger lift.
- Central heating throughout.
- Ironing facilities for guests' use.
- Garage or parking.
- Conference facilities for 10 or more persons.
- Establishment may be suitable for physically handicapped persons.
- Games room.
- Indoor swimming pool.
- Outdoor swimming pool.
- Tennis court(s).
- Riding and/or pony trekking at establishment or nearby.
- Private fishing rights.
- Golf (establishment's own golf course or arrangements at a course nearby).
- * Garden of ½ acre or more.
- Dogs NOT accepted.
- OAP Old age pensioners given reduced rates in low season.
- Building of notable historic/literary or architectural interest.
- T Bookings can be made through most recognised travel agents and booking agencies.

The following apply specifically to self-catering and camping caravan sites.

- M Gas/electricity or other fuel supply is by coin meter or meter reading.
- Electric cooking.
- Gas cooking.
- GE Gas/electric fires.
- Clothes washing machine and drying facilities.
- Refrigerator.
- Electric shaver points.
- LN Visitors must provide own linen.
- LF Linen provided free of charge.
- LH Linen hire service available.
- S Daily cleaning service.
- Telephone.
- * Garden.
- Hot water to all washbasins (caravan/camp sites).
- Showers.
- GAS Gas cylinder exchange or refill.
- Cafe or restaurant.
- Foodshop or mobile foodshop.
- Evening entertainment.
- Cinema and/or theatre.
- Children's playground.
- Water skiing.
- Boating.
- Sailing.

Self-catering Accommodation **CROMER**

Avenue Holiday Flats APPROVED

Comfortable, spacious, individually centrally heated self-contained flats in quiet area. Short distance from all amenities. Colour TV, washing machine, log burning stoves, private parking. Ground floor accommodation available. Short winter breaks. Discounts for long lets and couples. Owners resident on premises.

EATB Approved.
Sleeping: 4

Open January–December *Map B, Ref No. 4*

Barn Cottage APPROVED

Norfolk flint cottage, retaining several original features, in excellent decorative order throughout. Lovely position for walks to nearby cliffs, golf course and woods. Sea 10 mins easy walk. Good local shops nearby. Owners resident next door.

Sleeping: 4–5

Open May–October *Map B, Ref No. 18*

Beverley Holiday Flats APPROVED

Luxury Apartments for Non-Smokers

Winners of Award for Excellence
Spacious centrally heated self-contained apartments for **non-smokers**. 2–3 people. Furnished and equipped to high standard. No pets or young children. Ground floor accommodation available.

EATB Member
Sleeping: 3

Open April–October *Map B, Ref No. 35*

Brynor Holiday House

Runton Road, Cromer

Three bedroomed house with fine sea views plus lounge, sun-lounge, dining room, kitchen. Central heating, garage, enclosed garden. Personal supervision and well recommended.

Sleeping: 6

Open April–December *Map B, Ref No.45*

Cliff Avenue

Situated in a pleasant avenue close to the seafront, shops and other amenities. Accommodation – 2 flats – of a high standard in a detached older house of quality. Equally suitable for high summer holidays or spring, autumn and winter breaks.

Sleeping: 2–5

Open All year *Map B, Ref No. 31*

Cottage Holidays

Cambridge St., Cromer

Six nicely furnished 1, 2 and 3 bedroom cottages. Accommodation of a very high standard, maintained and supervised by ourselves. In quiet area of town centre, 2 minutes to beach, park and all amenities. Private car park.

Sleeping: 2–6

Open May–October *Map B, Ref No. 18*

HOLIDAY PRICES

	29 December–6 April 6 October–28 December			7 April–18 May 22 September–5 October			19 May–15 June 8 September–21 September			16 June–6 July	7 July–7 September
It is always advisable to check prices when booking	7 nights from/to	3 nights Fri–Sun from	4 nights Mon–Thu from	7 nights from/to	3 nights Fri–Sun from	4 nights Mon–Thu from	7 nights from/to	3 nights Fri–Sun from	4 nights Mon–Thu from	7 nights from/to	7 nights from/to
Avenue Holiday Flats	£48–£68	£38	£40	£65–£90			£85–£95			£95–£110	£95–£150
Barn Cottage				£130–£160			£150–£195			£175–£195	£195–£240
Beverley Holiday Flats				£85–£95			£95–£105			£105–£115	£115–£125
Brynor Holiday House	£80–£100	£50	£60	£100			£120			£120–£150	£150–£190
Cliff Avenue	£45–£80			£55–£90			£68–£110			£80–£120	£85–£165
Cottage Holidays	£55–£80	£40–£50	£45	£55–£115	£40	£45	£50–£150			£95–£175	£125–£190

Prices may not apply at Bank Holidays.

SECTION B

Choose ***one*** *of the following writing tasks. Your answer should follow* ***exactly*** *the instructions given. You are advised to write approximately 250 words.*

1 Write an article entitled 'The Pleasures of Gardening' for a magazine designed for general interest weekend reading. Most of the readers will not be especially interested in gardening and will need a lively article to get them started.

2 You have just witnessed a road accident involving one or two cars and a motorcycle. Write a detailed report about what occurred and how or why it happened. The police will use your report to help them decide who was to blame or how the particular road or junction could be improved.

3 While travelling on a bus you see a notice inviting passengers to give their views on how the service could be made more comfortable or convenient. Write a letter to the bus company giving your own ideas and opinions.

4 A friend who has just gone away to college writes and asks how you keep so fit. Perhaps the question surprises you, since you certainly aren't a fitness expert. However, you write to give your friend your advice and ideas on keeping fit and healthy at college.

PAPER 3 ENGLISH IN USE 1 hour 30 minutes

SECTION A

1 *Read the article below and for questions* ***1-16*** *circle the letter next to the word which best fits each space. The first answer has been given as an example.*

A LONG WAY ROUND

I knew the town quite well but I had to ask for instructions as to how to get to a particular restaurant. The instructions were easy to **(1)** . . . as the route was made up of three segments with each of which I was **(2)** . . . , for each of them **(3)** . . . some obvious landmark.

One day some friends set out for the restaurant from the same place as myself and at the **(4)** . . . time. But they got there **(5)** . . . before I did. I asked them if they had driven quickly but they **(6)** . . . this. Then I asked them what **(7)** . . . they had taken. They explained, and it was **(8)** . . . that they had taken a short cut. A small side turning had led them **(9)** . . . to the restaurant while I was making an unnecessary **(10)** . . . through the centre of the town.

My own route had always seemed satisfactory so I had never **(11)** . . . for a shorter one. In fact I was **(12)** . . . that a shorter one existed. I had driven past the small side turning each time, but had never **(13)** . . . it because there had never been any reason to do so, and I had never **(14)** . . . out how useful it was. My **(15)** . . . instructions had been in terms of large, well-known segments of route, because that is the easiest way to give instructions. There had never been any **(16)** . . . to find a better alternative.

1	A	pursue	(B)	follow	C	comply	D	take
2	A	aware	B	known	C	familiar	D	amazed
3	A	showed	B	displayed	C	passed	D	involved
4	A	similar	B	exact	C	very	D	same
5	A	long	B	much	C	rather	D	soon
6	A	denied	B	refused	C	rejected	D	disbelieved
7	A	way	B	map	C	journey	D	route
8	A	obvious	B	evidence	C	seen	D	unmistakable
9	A	punctually	B	directly	C	shortly	D	fast
10	A	tour	B	route	C	way	D	detour
11	A	looked	B	sought	C	tried	D	wanted
12	A	unknown	B	uninformed	C	unconcerned	D	unaware
13	A	sighted	B	found	C	explored	D	viewed
14	A	made	B	found	C	tried	D	turned
15	A	original	B	starting	C	first	D	friends'
16	A	purpose	B	reason	C	point	D	good

2 *Complete the following article by writing the missing words in the spaces provided. Use* ***only one word*** *in each space.*

FIRE: PLANNING AN ESCAPE ROUTE

Take a deliberate walk around your home. Stand in each room and consider how you would **(1)** __________ safely from it if there were a fire. Work out **(2)** __________ best route and an alternative if that should be blocked. Remember that you **(3)** __________ have to escape in the dark.

The most lethal element in a fire is smoke, **(4)** __________ flames. Shut the door where a fire **(5)** __________ started, to hold back the smoke. Even a small initial fire may develop rapidly and the smoke created **(6)** __________ be fatal.

You should establish some form **(7)** __________ fire drill, and choose an assembly point outside and **(8)** __________ away from the house. **(9)** __________ a routine tour of the house before **(10)** __________ to bed every night, to check that **(11)** __________ is safe. Switch off and unplug the TV. Check that heaters are safe and cookers switched **(12)** __________, and unplug electrical appliances. Make **(13)** __________ that no smouldering cigarette ends have **(14)** __________ left, and that doors and windows are firmly **(15)** __________.

SECTION B

3 *In most lines of the following text there is* **one** *unnecessary word. It is either grammatically incorrect or does not suit the sense of the text.*

Read the text, put a line through each unnecessary word and then write the word in the space provided at the end of the line. Some lines are correct. Indicate these lines with a tick (✔) against the line number. The first two lines have been done as examples.

FROM THE COURSE DIRECTOR

Welcome to the writers' course. You are about to take the	1	✔
second step in your writing career (~~you~~ having taken the	2	you
first step when you sent in your enrolment form). Yes, it	3	
now is the time to send to me the questionnaire giving	4	
details about yourself. I must have this before you start up	5	
your course. It will enable me to appoint the right tutor for	6	
you, to ensure you receive professional guidance in the	7	
writing speciality of your choice. In the months to come ahead	8	
your tutor will show you how to open the doors of your mind	9	
and shake out your hidden talents. You will learn how to trans-	10	
late your thoughts, views and the experiences into written	11	
works, how to select the right points to use them in your	12	
articles, fiction or telescripts, but how to put them together	13	
into saleable manuscripts bearing *your* name as author.	14	
Good luck with your work! I wish you a success!	15	

4 *You are a secretary, and your boss has asked you to write a formal letter to the painter, Bob Jones, basing what you say on her informal note below.*

Your formal letter to the painter is on the opposite page. Write the missing words in the spaces provided on the right. Use **not more than two words** *in each space.*

I'm sorry to say that I'm not too happy with the work Bob Jones has done just lately. The paint on my ceiling is very thin, so bits of last year's paint are still showing. Also, some of the paint on the walls is already flaking off — it looks really awful. So we'd better give him a couple of weeks to put things right. Otherwise we'll have to get someone else to do it, in which case we'll ask Jones to pay the bill!

Dear Mr Jones I (1) . . . to say that we are not entirely (2) . . . with the (3) . . . of your (4) . . . work. The paint which you have (5) . . . to the ceilings is very thin, and as a (6) . . . there are places where the (7) . . . coat of paint is plainly (8) . . . . In (9) . . . some of the paint on the walls is flaking off in an (10) . . . manner. I must (11) . . . to ask you to (12) . . . your work within the next (13) . . . . (14) . . . this, we shall be . . . (15) . . . to have it done at your (16)	1 ______ 9 ______ 2 ______ 10 ______ 3 ______ 11 ______ 4 ______ 12 ______ 5 ______ 13 ______ 6 ______ 14 ______ 7 ______ 15 ______ 8 ______ 16 ______

SECTION C

5 *Choose the best phrase or sentence (given below the text) to fill each of the blanks in the following text. Write one letter (**A-G**) in each of the numbered spaces. Two of the suggested answers do not fit at all.*

CARS AND SOCIETY

Nowadays just over half of all households in Britain have one or more cars. The increasing use of cars has had an enormous effect on society, health, the landscape and other aspects of life. In the 19th century railways caused workers in other transport industries to lose their jobs, but they also employed a great many people. In the twentieth century, railway workers lost their jobs as roads provided more employment.

(1) __________, and have opened up whole areas which were formerly inaccessible. Country parks, stately homes and other attractions often depend on access by car, for public transport rarely serves them.

(2) __________. As late as the 1950s almost every district had a number of corner shops. People used these shops for almost all the things they needed each day such as food, papers and household goods. They would have gone into town to visit the market and purchase items unobtainable locally perhaps only once or twice a month. Daily shopping was done within the local community, and the meetings with other people kept the community going.

(3) __________, travelling further than before and going by car if possible. The use of a car makes the journey easy and means that they can bring back enough shopping to last them a week or more. Cars have helped to drive many corner shops out of business.

(4) __________, but many towns and cities now have giant shops selling do-it-yourself materials, and these are often in 'out-of-town' centres or trading estates that are not served by bus. (5) __________.

Many other facilities also depend on improved road transport, often involving the use of cars. Modern hospitals, schools, libraries and other instutitions are often built to serve large areas. Compared with those which they have replaced they are fewer, larger and more remote from the people who use them.

A However, many railways have been improved

B They depend on customers having cars

C Modern town-dwellers like to have private transport

D Nowadays, a large percentage of people do their shopping at supermarkets

E Nearly all shopping centres can be reached by bus as well as car

F Increased mobility, mainly by car, also leads to facilities closing

G In general, cars have increased people's chances of travelling for pleasure

6 *Your flatmate Mary is going to run a charity stall at a market. Her friend John rings when she is out and you note what he says. Turn your notes into an informal letter to leave for your friend.*

You must use all the words in the same order as the notes. You may add words and change the form of words where necessary. Look carefully at the example which has been done for you.

a Can help with stall but can't carry (backache).

b Wants to know how get to market – his car, or yours repaired?

c Also, what time start and finish? Early if wet?

d Can donate old bike – squeaky, brakes good.

e If car not needed can ride it here Sat.

f Really keen – thinks stall gt success.

g Worried 2 helpers not enough. Hope 100s customers!

h Peter help? Very strong – can carry.

i If Peter, no trouble thieves (usually serious problem markets).

Dear Mary

John rang at six o'clock.

a *He can help with the stall but he can't do any carrying because of his backache*

b ______________________________

____

c ______________________________

d ______________________________

e ______________________________

f ______________________________

g ______________________________

h ______________________________

i ______________________________

Perhaps you'd better ring him back.

Best wishes,

Judy

TEST THREE

PAPER 4 LISTENING 35 minutes

SECTION A

*You will hear a tape of a radio broadcast. It describes the past and present use of sites and buildings in the town of Morley. You will find that most have changed their function over the years. Listen to the recording and answer questions **1-10** by completing the table. Use no more than three words per answer. You will hear the piece twice.*

EARLIER USE		PRESENT USE	
	Quarry	1	
2			Factory and cafe
3			Bypass road
	Park with trees	4	
5			Recreation ground
6			Park
	Church	7	
	Prison	8	
	School	9	
10			Library

SECTION B

You will hear someone giving a message over the telephone. As you listen fill in the information for questions 11-26.

Listen carefully as you will hear the piece ONLY ONCE.

Telephone Message

Time: 10.30 am
Date: Thursday 1st
From: Miss Birch, Well-Tuned Autos Ltd
To: J. Wiggins

(1) Your car is nearly ready but your **11** ______ haven't been seen to. Replacing the **12** ______ would bring the cost to over **13** ______ . Could you ring about this? But you can collect the car now if you need it **14** ______ .

(2) The garage have noticed some **15** ______ – I think it's **16** ______ the car and not in the bodywork. They say it would cost **17** ______ to repair. Miss Birch will **18** ______ if she's there, but if she's at **19** ______ there will only be a **20** ______ . She says the rust will **21** ______ of your car – it may only last for **22** ______ .

(3) Your bill isn't quite correct. They've mixed up the sums for **23** ______ and **24** ______ but the **25** ______ is correct. She says it's come out of the **26** ______ like that and she hopes you won't mind.

Received by: Jack

SECTION C

You are going to hear an exchange between two speakers. One, Mr Burkiss, has recently had his car removed from his drive in the night. For questions **27-37** *choose the answer you think fits best by indicating the letter* **A**, **B**, **C** *or* **D** *against the number of each question. Give* **one answer only** *to each question.*

You will hear the piece twice.

27 The night Mr Burkiss's car disappeared

A he woke up but saw nothing going on in his drive.
B he did not wake up.
C he woke up but only saw a dog or a cat.
D he woke up and saw that his car had gone.

28 Mr Burkiss refers to burglaries

A only in his own road.
B in his own road and other nearby streets.
C only in other nearby streets.
D in his district or neighbourhood without being more precise about where.

29 The other speaker thinks Mr Burkiss was 'criminal' to leave the car unlocked because

A he feels that carelessly helping criminals is almost as bad as crime itself.
B Mr Burkiss was helping his brother, a car thief.
C it was part of a plan to cheat the insurance company.
D it was part of his plan to make a quick getaway.

30 The other speaker knows Mr Burkiss has obtained a form recently because

A he must have used the previous form when he damaged the car three years ago.
B the form is a new kind.
C his broker remembers giving it to him recently.
D the car is only two months old.

31 The other speaker thinks Mr Burkiss failed to lock his car

A because he was careless.
B to make things easier for his brother.
C because he trusted his lights to scare off thieves.
D because he didn't want the bother of unlocking it when he was in a hurry.

32 The conversation seems to be taking place

A in a court or police station.
B as part of a television programme about crime.
C as part of a conversation in the street.
D between an insurance company's customer and one of its representatives.

SECTION D

Now look at Section D for the last part of the test. You will hear various people talking about winter.

TASK ONE lists the particular things which people are talking about. Indicate the order in which you hear them by writing a number from 1–5 in each box.. Three boxes will remain empty.

TASK 1

Party time	33	
Keeping warm	34	
Road conditions	35	
Protecting plants	36	
Playing in snow	37	
The weather	38	
Harvesting vegetables	39	
Growing old	40	

TASK TWO lists the people you hear speaking in the five extracts. Indicate the order in which you hear them by writing a number from 1-5 in each box. Three boxes will remain empty.

You will hear the series twice.

TASK 2

Taxi driver	41	
Child or teenager	42	
Invalid	43	
Mother	44	
People shopping	45	
Expert gardener	46	
Bus driver	47	
Farm worker(s)	48	

TEST THREE

PAPER 5 SPEAKING 15 minutes

QUESTION 1 *(candidate 1)*

The examiner will ask you to describe the photograph on page 90 to your partner, who has a photograph which is related to yours in some way.

At the end of one minute the examiner will ask your partner to say what the relationship between your pictures is. You should then try to reach agreement with your partner.

NB: The instructions would not appear on the examination material in the real exam. They would be conveyed orally by the examiner.

QUESTION 1 *(candidate 2)*

The examiner will ask your partner to describe a photograph to you. The photograph on page 94 is related to your partner's in some way.

After one minute you may ask short questions if you wish or find it necessary. The examiner will then ask you to say what the relationship between the photographs is. You should then try to reach agreement with your partner.

QUESTION 2 *(candidate 1)*

The examiner will ask your partner to describe one of the six photographs below to you.

At the end of one minute the examiner will ask you to say which photograph your partner was describing.

QUESTION 2 *(candidate 2)*

The examiner will ask you to describe one of the six photographs below to your partner (who has the same six photographs).

At the end of one minute the examiner will ask your partner to say which photograph you were describing.

QUESTION 3 *(both candidates)*

Look at the set of cartoons.

Discuss with your partner what they show and what the artist is trying to say. You must either reach agreement or 'agree to disagree'. Make sure that you understand your partner's opinion. At the end of three minutes you will be asked to report your decision to the examiners, and take part in further discussions.

TEST FOUR

PAPER 1 READING 1 hour

FIRST TEXT QUESTIONS 1-7

These questions are based on an extract from a book.

*For questions **1-7** you must choose which of the extracts **A-H** on the following page match the numbered gaps in the text. There is one additional extract which does not belong in any of the gaps. Indicate your answers* ***on the separate answer sheet.***

Art Revelations

For centuries, the world's most famous painting has been Leonardo da Vinci's portrait of a woman, known as the Mona Lisa, which hangs in the Louvre Museum in Paris. For almost as long, the identity of the sitter has been the art world's most celebrated mystery.

1	

It was always assumed that it was indeed of Lisa (more commonly known as La Giaconda) because Vasari, the world's first art historian, said so in his *Lives of the artists*. But this was hearsay, since the book was not published until the mid-1540s, when Leonardo had been dead for more than 20 years. Vasari himself had never so much as seen the painting. Leading scholars have therefore argued – and in certain cases fervently urged – that the Louvre painting might well depict some other rich lady.

2	

The man, known as Salai, was an apprentice in the master's studio from the age of 10. When Salai died, a few years after Leonardo, his two sisters fought over his will, and it became the subject of a court action. The will is among the records of this which have now been discovered in Milan.

3	

One was a portrait of someone called Leda. Another depicted 'La Gioconda', and there seems little doubt that this was the portrait known as the Mona Lisa today.

4	

It was evidently painted at the turn of the sixteenth century, rather than some years later, as art historians had sometimes supposed.

5	

The discovery proves that Leonardo's paintings were already highly prized in his lifetime, and that they did not pass directly to France but to Leonardo's fellow Italians. People would have come from all round Milan to copy his work, both before his death and afterwards. The paintings must have been bought by the French at a later date.

6	

Whereas some paintings in the will are valued at 25 lire, the three Leonardos were given values ranging from 500 to more than 1000 lire. This was equivalent to the price of a reasonable sized house in Milan – the equivalent of a £500,000 London house or a New York apartment today. The prices certainly prove that the paintings were originals and not just copies.

7	

It has always been known that Leonardo made drawings for a 'Leda' painting, but no such painting has survived, and people have doubted that Leonardo ever completed it. However, the Leda in the Milan will was valued at 1,010 lire, far too much for a drawing, even by such a great master. Perhaps someone, somewhere, has a valuable Leda by Leonardo and does not know it . . .

A The discovery is important because knowing the subject's identity helps in dating the painting.

B There has never been any concrete evidence that the picture was of Lisa, wife of Francesco del Giocondo, a Florentine merchant.

C The will, to be published in next month's Burlington Magazine, shows that Salai owned three valuable paintings which Leonardo had left him.

D The will puts a truly startling value on Leonardo's canvasses.

E But the discovery also presents another, perhaps more tantalising mystery.

F But now two scholars – an American and an Italian – working in the state archives in Milan, have discovered the will of a man who had been a member of Leonardo's household.

G The will also clears up another mystery – why, if the paintings were taken from Leonardo's house to the French Royal collection, there are so many copies in northern Italy.

H A computer analysis of the image, carried out last year in the United States, even concluded that the painting showed a man disguised as a woman.

SECOND TEXT QUESTIONS 8-15

Read this extract, which comes from a magazine called 'Which?' For questions 8-15 you must choose the answer which you think best completes each unfinished question or statement about the text. ***On your answer sheet****, indicae the letter A, B, C or D against the number of each question. Give* ***one answer only*** *to each question.*

What's Wrong With *Ca$h* Machines?

MECHANICAL PROBLEMS

Putting a card into a machine to get cash sounds a simple enough operation. But with an average of 5,000 withdrawals every month from each cash dispenser, things can, and do, go badly wrong.

Our survey showed that over a third of you had at some time had your card swallowed by a cash dispenser for no apparent reason – in one worrying case, the cash dispenser spat the card back out five minutes later. The usual reason for this indigestion is that the magnetic strip on the card has been damaged, either by wear and tear or by a magnetic object 'scrambling' the coded information. Don't leave your card near large electrical goods such as washing machines – when they're turned on, the magnetic field can easily scramble the card's strip.

TIP

Magnetic strips are often damaged when the card is bent, or the strip is scratched by keys or coins, so don't carry your cards around loose. And be careful not to put two cards back to back – it could scramble *both* strips.

Another, less common, problem is when the cash dispenser gets its sums wrong. Six per cent of you have been given the wrong amount of money on at least one occasion. Five per cent have been given no cash at all, despite your account being debited, and one per cent have been given money for nothing, having made withdrawals which have never appeared on your statements.

The main reason for this is that new bank notes can either bunch together or jam in the note feeder. The banks say that it's possible to tell when someone's been given the wrong money in 'virtually all' cases – but be on your guard.

TIP

Count your money as soon as you get it. If you're given the wrong amount of cash, or no cash at all, make an immediate note of what happened, including the exact time of the withdrawal and the location of the cash dispenser. Keep any receipt. If there's someone in the queue behind you, get their name and address and ask them to witness the note. Complain to the bank, building society or shop where the dispenser is located as soon as possible. Copy the letter to your own bank or building society. And, of course, always check your bank statements.

PHANTOM WITHDRAWALS

Your bank statement shows a cash dispenser withdrawal which you *know* you haven't made. You haven't told anyone your PIN (Personal Identification Number), and anyway you know that the card was in your possession at the time.You complain. Your bank says that the only possible explanation is that you're mistaken. It's up to you to prove the bank wrong, but how?

'Phantom withdrawals' are very rare in terms of the overall number of withdrawals from cash dispensers. But they're very unpleasant if you're the victim.

Most phantom withdrawals take place within a few miles of the cardholder's home or workplace. The most likely source of these withdrawals is that someone has seen you key in your PIN, or knows where you've written it down, and has 'borrowed' the card.

TIP

Don't leave your card lying around, never tell anyone your PIN and *never* write it down. One newspaper recently advised readers to 'disguise' their PINs if they wrote them down by, for example, adding one to each digit. Our advice is DON'T DO IT – a thief could crack a code like this in seconds.

PINNING THE BLAME

However, the borrowed card theory isn't the only possible explanation for phantom withdrawals. The banks' assumption that you're in the wrong hinges on the fact that only you and the bank's computer know your PIN, so any withdrawal made using your card and PIN is entirely your responsibility. But we're not convinced.

Since the banks own, operate and profit from the cash dispensers, we think it should be up to *them* to prove that everything was working perfectly when the withdrawal took place. *None* of the card contracts that we looked at states that the bank will do this.

But even this wouldn't solve the problem completely. The banks can still argue that you told someone else your PIN, or wrote it down somewhere – which is impossible for you to disprove.

The banks know that some people find PINs hard to remember, particularly if they have several cards. We think they should work towards a safer system, such as fingerprint authentication.

> IN BRIEF
>
> To get your money from a card machine someone has to insert your card and type in your PIN. Keep them both to yourself!

● *Credit due*

When Gerry Healey used a cash dispenser to pay £32.48 into his Abbeylink account, he was disconcerted when his receipt recorded the credit – but showed a £1.09 *reduction* in his account balance. And he was seriously worried when his statement didn't show the transaction. Abbey National blamed 'data corruption' and refunded the money.

Gerry's experience isn't an isolated case. For example, another reader, Mr Young, tried to transfer £900 between accounts using a Midland cash dispenser. The transfer showed on the receipts – but not on his statement.

● *Short-changed*

Eric Bedford inserted his Co-operative bank card in a Halifax cash dispenser and requested £50. The machine gave him a receipt but not cash. After Eric had complained, a woman who had overheard his conversation came up and gave him £50. She had been next in line to use the cash dispenser, asked for £30 and received £80.

Eric wrote to the Co-operative asking what would have happened if the next person in line hadn't been so honest? The bank told Eric that "it is *very likely* that you would have been refunded with the £50 you so nearly lost'. But not, Eric noted, guaranteed.

●

When Mrs A opened her bank statements, she saw cash dispenser withdrawals totalling around £4,000, which she knew the hadn't made. Mrs A kept her cashcard in a drawer at home, and her PIN was hidden in her jewellery box. She was adamant that she had *never* used a cash dispenser.

In desperation, she complained to the Banking Ombudsman. But after the Ombudsman had started his investigation, Mrs A asked him to drop the case – she suspected that a relative had found her card and PIN and made the 'phantom' withdrawals.

---

8 Cash machines keep people's cards

A for no real reason at all.
B because the machine has damaged the card.
C because of 'mechanical problems' inside the machine.
D because the card-holder has damaged the magnetic strip on the back of the card.

9 Customers can get the wrong amount of money through

A notes getting bunched together or jammed.
B data getting corrupted (or muddled), as in Gerry Healey's case.
C the cash card having been damaged beforehand.
D the machine's 'magic eye' miscounting the notes as they are dispensed.

10 If the machine you are using gives you the wrong amount of money you should

A get the name and address of any witness.
B check your bank statements.
C find out whether someone has 'borrowed' your card.
D complain at the place where the cash machine is and make a copy of the letter they send to your bank or building society.

11 Mrs A's 'phantom withdrawals' were typical because

A she had kept her card and PIN number secret.
B she knew she had never used a cash machine.
C she had been cheated by someone who had used her card and PIN number.
D she had left her card where it could easily be damaged by keys or other sharp objects.

12 Which of the following would make the best title for the passage about Mrs A?

A A good place to hide it.
B Not a phantom after all.
C Help from the Ombudsman.
D Never trust banks!

13 What struck Eric Bedford about his experience was that

A his bank was willing to refund lost money.
B his bank relied on its customers' honesty.
C his bank might or might not refund lost money.
D the woman had been exceptionally honest.

14 The article says it is up to the banks

A to ensure that machines are working properly.
B to know of virtually every case of customers getting the wrong amount of money.
C to trust their customers unless they are caught out by fingerprint evidence.
D to prove their case in any dispute.

15 The article advises people

A not to let two cards come into contact with one another.
B never to write their PIN number down unless they disguise it really well.
C not to let their cards get damaged in washing machines.
D to arm themselves with evidence if things go wrong.

THIRD TEXT QUESTIONS 16-32

Answer these questions by referring to the magazine article called 'Gardeners' Puzzles' below.

*Questions **16-32** ask you about the conditions which affect the growth of different kinds of plants, and **A–J** list these conditions.* ***On your answer sheet****, indicate your answers to each question by choosing from the list.*

Note: *Where more than one answer is needed you may give the answers* ***in any order.***

What conditions do most garden plants need? **16** .... **17** **18**	**A** lime or chalk
What conditions do lettuces and cabbages need? **19**	**B** suitable companion plants
What conditions do nasturtiums need? **20** **21**	**C** moving water
What does watercress need? **22** **23**	**D** sun
Where do water lilies grow? **24**	**E** dry soil
What do watercress and wallflowers both like? **25**	**F** moist soil
What do cabbages need? **26** **27**	**G** still water
What do carrots need? **28** **29**	**H** rich soil
What causes carrots to grow in odd shapes? **30**	**I** fresh manure
What do tomatoes need to grow well? **31** **32**	**J** lots of shade

Gardeners' Puzzles

What to grow where – this is the question which bedevils almost all amateur gardeners. Plants have their different likes and dislikes, which come in all sorts of combinations. Most, for example, like a sunny spot where the soil is rich and water-retentive. This is true – as a general rule – both for flowers and vegetables. However, there are lots of exceptions. While onions, tomatoes and marrows insist on their full sunshine quota, leaf vegetables, such as lettuces and cabbages, will usually tolerate partial shade, though they still insist on good, rich soil.

Turning to flowers, we quickly find that the usual love of sun and rich soil does not always apply. Some do best if they're positively starved of goodness and grown in arid, near-desert conditions. Nasturtiums, for example, flower most freely in parched, sandy soil which would be the death of most other plants. They bask beneath a blazing sun and they don't even ask for a cooling drink! If you make the mistake of giving nasturtiums water – and plant food – they'll pay you back by growing leaves instead of flowers.

And it's hard to make sense of all these botanical preferences. Nasturtiums are related to watercress, but though they belong to the same plant family their water needs are totally different. Unlike nasturtiums, watercress needs to be swamped in water – but does it need moving water or a stagnant pond? Well, the answer, if you want to know, is that watercress only grows in streams (it's water *lilies* that grow in ponds) and there needs to be lots of chalk or lime dissolved in the water.

If watercress needs water do wallflowers need walls? The quick answer is no, they don't need walls, but they do get their name from their habit of colonising crumbling walls when they get the chance. One of the nicest sights is to see a crumbling church tower with its south-facing aspect smothered – especially at the higher levels – with masses of wallflowers growing wild. Wallflowers, you see, obey the rule that flowers need sun to do really well; but they aren't so bothered about moist conditions or good rich soil, though they do like the lime they find in the mortar between the bricks or stones of a wall.

It's surprising to find that wallflowers belong to the cabbage family, despite the fact that the two are as different as chalk and cheese – or at any rate as different as nasturtiums and watercress. Cabbages *don't* insist on sun, but they do like moist, really fertile soil with lots of well-rotted manure. Carrots actually *like* to be in a gloomy spot and they like lots of nourishment in the soil – but beware of digging in fresh manure just before you sow the seed. If you make this mistake you'll get some very odd-shaped results. Instead, sow your carrots in soil that was well manured the previous season – unless you're one of those people who delight in growing freak vegetables.

One final surprise: potatoes and tomatoes are another oddly-matched couple that come from the same plant family. You can see the link if you study the leaves, which are very similar. Or look at the little berries that grow on potato plants. Don't eat them though – the berries we get from tomato plants are full of vitamins, but the ones we get from the closely-related potato are thoroughly unfit to eat. And as usual, the plants have different needs: the potato simply doesn't share the tomato's greedy sunshine requirements. Nor does it share the tomato's mysterious love for French marigolds. Pair them up in the same bed or border and see your tomatoes grow like mad!

FOURTH TEXT QUESTIONS 33-46

Answer the following questions by referring to the extract from a Nutrition advice booklet on page 74.

These questions ask you to choose the correct title for each section (1-5). ***A-H*** *list the possible titles.* ***On your answer sheet*** *indicate the answer to each question by choosing from the list* ***A-H.***

33	Section 1	A	Vital fluids
34	Section 2	B	Paid in Salt
35	Section 3	C	It's All a Matter of Taste
36	Section 4	D	How Much is Safe?
37	Section 5	E	Roles of Salt in the Body
		F	Do We Need to Cut Down?
		G	Chemicals in Food
		H	Uses of Salt

*These questions ask you about the substances mentioned in the text. On your answer sheet indicate your answers to questions **38-42** by choosing from the list **I-L**, and indicate your answers to **43-46** by choosing from the list **M-O**. You may have to make one or two of the choices* **more than once**.

***Note**: When a question asks for more than one answer you may give the answers* **in any order**.

What does sodium do in the body? **38** .... **39** .... **40** .... What does chlorine do in the body? **41** **42**	**I** helps nerves to function **J** controls level of body fluids **K** influences blood pressure **L** contributes to digestive fluid
What does salt do in cheese? **43** .... **44** .... What does salt do in meat? **45** .... What does salt do in bread? **46**	**M** affects the texture **N** helps to stop it going bad **O** contributes to the flavour

Salt

①

Salt is a naturally occurring compound which is made up of the ions of two elements, sodium ions and chloride ions (approximately 40% sodium and 60% chloride), hence its chemical name 'Sodium Chloride'. Salt is present in the sea, rocks, sand and also many foods both of animal and vegetable origin. It is an important body fluid constituent and, in small amounts, an essential dietary requirement.

The word 'salt' is believed to be derived from the word 'salary', which is thought to come from the Latin word 'salarius', meaning 'salt money'. Salt used to be a means of payment years ago, and in many countries it was rare, and therefore a prized food ingredient. It is also said by others to be derived from 'Sal', a Roman Goddess of Health. Whichever is true, salt was a valued and important substance.

②

Salt has many functions in food which include:

Preservative, for example, in cured meats, where it reduces the moisture level available for the growth of certain undesirable micro-organisms. These micro-organisms, including many bacteria, may otherwise cause food spoilage and possible ill health.

Textural agent, as is the case, when added during the production of cheese and bread. In breadmaking, salt plays an important role by assisting the development of gluten. (Gluten is the main protein in wheat which influences the dough's elasticity), and in cheese salt influences the final texture.

Flavours and Flavour enhancers Flavours naturally present in foods may be enhanced or emphasised by the addition of a little salt. In other cases, salt contributes to the characteristic flavour (e.g. in salted nuts, cheese and crisps).

③

Approximately 10% of sodium is found in tissue cells, 40% is present in bone cells and the remaining 50% will be located outside cells (mainly in body fluids). Sodium is required for nerve and muscle functioning and the control of body fluids. It is a major factor determining blood volume and blood pressure.

The requirement for water and salt are closely related. Too little salt may result in muscular cramps and high salt intakes are likely to cause a feeling of thirst.
Loss of fluid in perspiration (e.g. after strenuous exercise or in a hot climate) elevates the concentration of sodium in the remaining body fluid. The consequence of the raised sodium concentration is a feeling of thirst and a subsequent drink will compensate for the fluid lost.

Chlorine plays an important part in digestion because it is a major element in the acid present in our stomachs, and like sodium it is essential for correct functioning of the nervous system.

④

Our present consumption in the United Kingdom is thought to be approximately 9 to 12 grams of salt per day. It is believed that between 3 and 8 grams should be more than enough for most people. 3 to 8 grams represent about ˘ to 1˘ level teaspoons. Lower intakes may result in food not being acceptable to our conditioned palates. This includes the sodium and chlorine naturally present in foods and drink as well as salt added at the table or in cooking.

It is unlikely that we would suffer from a deficiency of salt if we did not use it when cooking, as there is sufficient present in many foods.

⑤

Many studies have shown that individuals who have very high blood pressure, or whose family, especially parents or grandparents, have high blood pressure, may benefit by controlling their salt intake. To date the emphasis has been mainly on the restriction of sodium. Some medical experts believe that replacing sodium with potassium by, for example, using potassium-based salt substitutes may be beneficial. This would still allow a 'salty' taste to be enjoyed by individuals who are recommended to reduce their sodium intake.
If a doctor has advised a reduction in salt, it is wise to check whether or not salt substitutes would be permitted.
High blood pressure is one of the many risk factors of heart disease and it is more prevalent in overweight persons. Weight reduction can often bring about a fall in blood pressure.
For normally healthy individuals who have no family history of high blood pressure, it is generally felt that reducing salt intake may not necessarily be of benefit, but it is believed that, in the majority of cases, it would do no harm.

TEST FOUR

PAPER 2 WRITING 2 hours

SECTION A

You are looking for a summer job before going to college to take a management course. The following advertisement has appeared in a local paper, and you think that the job might be suitable for you, in spite of one or two reservations which you have. You have made a few notes on the advertisement, and you have also made some other notes about yourself. Using the information and ideas provided, write a letter applying for the job and asking any relevant questions.

You may invent any extra details to complete your answer but **do not change** *any of the information given.*

You are advised to write approximately 250 words.

WANTED

Working hours?

Fit young man or woman (preferably 16-25 years old) to supervise garage forecourt during the summer months. This is a serve-yourself petrol station, normally open round the clock and unattended for most of the year. In summer, the pressure of customers raises minor problems (such as shortage of change, occasional broken-down vehicles needing to be pushed clear) which the supervisor must try to resolve. In addition, some foreign customers need advice in working the pumps, and a knowledge of foreign languages would therefore be useful. ← travelled lots in Middle East

The job requires initiative, a friendly manner and ability to cope under pressure or during long slack periods. It is hoped that the presence of an attendant will help to curb vandalism and pilfering. ← could be fun!

Mechanical knowledge is not required, but the applicant must be trustworthy and accurate in the handling of money. Oh dear!

Non-smoker essential, overalls supplied. ← Why?

Apply to Mr Wesley, King's Garage, Konigsberg.

(Pay?)

ME

Born 1974

Good exam passes in maths, English, French, art

Shop work during previous holidays

First aid and swimming certs

Like repairing cars — brother has garage

Free July — Sept.

SECTION B

*Choose **one** of the following writing tasks. Your answer should follow **exactly** the instructions given. You are advised to write approximately 250 words.*

1 Write a magazine article to introduce your hobby to people who know nothing about it.

2 A friend's child was hurt in a slight road accident while you were looking after him or her. You have taken the child to hospital, where he or she is now being treated for slight injuries. You cannot see your friend in person, so write a note to explain what has happened and express your regrets. Be frank but avoid causing undue alarm.

3 A friend wants to borrow your camera, or a piece of electrical equipment such as a video recorder. You cannot hand the equipment over in person, so write a note giving clear instructions for using it, and warn your friend of any danger or damage which could result if it is not used properly.

4 You were impressed – or very annoyed - by the standard of a recent television programme. Write a review of the programme, explaining how it struck you and what made it either good or bad.

PAPER 3 ENGLISH IN USE 1 hour 30 minutes

SECTION A

1 *Read the article below and for questions **1-16** circle the letter next to the word which best fits each space. The first answer has been given as an example.*

FREE INSPIRATION

Anybody with a real desire to write, plus an average vocabulary and enthusiasm, can be taught to write saleable short stories. Short story writing is not **(1)** . . . money, but it can be a delightful and remunerative hobby. And the beauty of it is that **(2)** . . . is all around us.

I know several writers who make notes not only of scenes and surroundings, but of **(3)** . . . . That does not mean that when they dine with the doctor they lift his **(4)** . . . word for the next story in which a **(5)** . . . character appears. It does not mean that they **(6)** . . . a notebook furtively under their soup-plate or scribble frantically behind their newspaper in a train. What it does mean is that their ears are open and their eyes **(7)** . . . for the apt phrase and the perfect setting, for the brilliant repartee and the characteristic **(8)** . . . .

You can sometimes be with a person for hours of uneventful conversation, and then suddenly he will say something or **(9)** . . . a gesture which will immediately **(10)** . . . in your mind a mental comment such as 'Nobody else would do that,' or 'Funny, that habit of his!'

It is those individual phrases, those **(11)** . . . gestures, those quaint bursts of speech or action, that make character. Thus it is that there are **(12)** . . . occasions when you can observe, and (if wise) later make a **(13)** . . . of, valuable material. Perhaps a hostess handles a tactless guest admirably; you hear a telling phrase in a sermon, **(14)** . . . a motor accident and see for yourself the **(15)** . . . of the shaken drivers, hear a business argument in the train.

(16) . . . the points down!

1	(A)	easy	B	ready	C	simple	D	vast
2	A	aspiration	B	inspiration	C	satisfaction	D	story-line
3	A	exchanges	B	talks	C	dialogues	D	conversations
4	A	every	B	very	C	each	D	final
5	A	clerical	B	healing	C	medical	D	medicinal
6	A	cram	B	jam	C	stuff	D	slip
7	A	bright	B	alert	C	active	D	peering
8	A	activity	B	gesture	C	sign	D	scenario
9	A	give	B	make	C	produce	D	raise
10	A	illicit	B	produce	C	rouse	D	spring
11	A	observant	B	partial	C	distinctive	D	distinguished
12	A	countless	B	uncounted	C	unknown	D	unrestricted
13	A	recording	B	list	C	note	D	memorandum
14	A	witness	B	scrutinise	C	sight	D	attend
15	A	activities	B	sayings	C	feelings	D	reactions
16	A	copy	B	set	C	record	D	jot

2 *Complete the following article, which is about selecting people to go on expeditions, by writing the missing words in the spaces provided. Use* ***only one word*** *in each space.*

BE PREPARED FOR THE WORST!

Expeditions into the wild are very demanding, and candidates have to show that they can fend for themselves in rugged countryside. They are divided **(1)** __________ teams and put through a series of physical tests **(2)** __________ a period of 36 hours. These normally **(3)** __________ following a route using a map and compass, crossing a river **(4)** __________ rope, abseiling, making a raft and **(5)**__________ crossing a lake or river on it. Even worse, candidates also **(6)** __________ to lead a blindfolded companion through a series of obstacles, measure an animal **(7)** __________ a dark room, or possibly weigh a snake, cook food on a camp fire, or deal **(8)** __________ a midnight emergency!

Because there may be long evenings with **(9)** __________ much to do in a remote part of the world, **(10)** __________ team must also invent and act out a short entertainment for other teams **(11)** __________ watch.

All the candidates are anonymous and are impartially assessed by an experienced panel **(12)** __________ judges. Successful candidates are those **(13)** __________ can meet a challenge happily, who show a potential for leadership, courage, patience and **(14)** __________ all friendliness. Usually about one third of those who go **(15)** __________ a selection weekend are chosen, but once it's over most people say they enjoyed the experience.

SECTION B

3 *In most lines of the following text there is* **one** *unnecessary word. It is either grammatically incorrect or it does not suit the sense of the text. Read the text, put a line through each unnecessary word and then put the word in the space provided at the end of the line. Some lines are correct. Indictate these lines with a tick (✔) against the line number. The first two lines have been done as examples.*

THE HONEY DANCE

Bees cannot talk so they dance instead. They do	1	✔
this to let each other ~~to~~ know where food can be	2	to
found. A dancing bee begins by running in a straight	3	
line, and as she does it so she waggles her body	4	
to attract the other bees' to attention. After	5	
going a certain distance along she turns to the	6	
left and hurries back to her starting point. Then	7	
she does her run again, but in this time she turns	8	
to the right at the end, and thus completing a	9	
sort of figure of eight. To human observers the	10	
dance lacks the meaning; to bees it is full of	11	
detail, and the detail is not only meaningful but	12	
vital to survival. It shows them which direction	13	
to take off and how far far to go to reach the	14	
flowers on which they depend on.	15	

4 *You work as an office manager for a typewriter company. A secretary has telephoned the Norwood Hotel in an effort to book a room where you can show prospective customers your latest models. The secretary has left a memo on your desk reporting on his or her conversation with the Hotel owner, Mr Briggs. You have rewritten the note for your boss's attention. Complete the note to your boss on page 80 by writing the missing words in the spaces provided on the right. The first answer has been given as an example.*

Use ***not more than two words*** *in each space.*

Got in touch with Mr Briggs at the Norwood to try and get a room for our typewriter demo. I'm sorry but Mr Briggs says he's fully booked this month. He says try the Montague – only just opened, so could do with the business and the manager there would probably knock something off the price.

Mr Briggs owns the Montague as well as the Norwood. He says we could move the bookings we already have to the Montague if we liked it more. Anyway, it's urgent to book for the typewriter demo. What shall I do?

We have (1) . . . Mr Briggs at the Norwood Hotel in (2) . . . to book a room for our (3) . . . of typewriters. (4) . . . , Mr Briggs (5) . . . accept a booking for the (6) . . . month . He (7) . . . us to try the Montague Hotel, which has opened (8) . . . . (9) . . . to Mr Briggs, they would (10) . . . the business, and the manager there would probably give us a (11) . . . .

Mr Briggs owns (12) . . . hotels and would let us transfer our (13) . . . bookings to the Montague Hotel if we (14) . . . it.

Booking for the typewriter demonstration is now a matter of (15) . . .. What (16) . . . would you like us to take?

1 contacted
2 ________
3 ________
4 ________
5 ________
6 ________
7 ________
8 ________
9 ________
10 ________
11 ________
12 ________
13 ________
14 ________
15 ________
16 ________

SECTION C

5 *Choose the best phrase or sentence (given below the text) to fill each of the blanks in the following text.*

*Write one letter (**A-G**) in each of the numbered spaces.*

Two of the suggested answers do not fit at all.

HURRICANE FORCE

The true hurricane must possess winds in excess of 112 kph, as well as the whirling spiral winds which make such impressive displays on photographs taken from space.

Hardly surprisingly, it is only very recently that weather men have been able to find out much about what makes a hurricane tick.

(1) ________, but studies have been made and are now, of course, aided by satellite pictures. The key feature of such an intense storm is the 'eye' at its centre, a region of relatively calm, warm and cloudless air from 15 to 60 km across, bounded by steep walls of cloud towering to heights as great as 10 km or more above sea level. **(2)** ________; the surrounding clouds are produced where air sweeping in from outside at sea level rises and spins round the eye. Such powerful updrafts produce dramatic cooling of the warm air, which is laden with moisture from the sea below, and the result is torrential rain. **(3)** ________, with winds often exceeding 160 kph.

Once the system is established, drawing energy from the warm ocean below, nothing can stop it until it reaches land, which cuts off the supply of water, or cooler water farther from the equator, which cuts off the supply of heat. The whole hurricane system may move at about 48 kph, generally giving ample time for it to be tracked and appropriate precautions to be taken in the region towards which it is headed. **(4)** ________, rainfall of 2.5 cm or more per hour, and the added risk of flooding from a rise in sea level produced by the very low pressure at the centre of the hurricane.

Although hurricanes generally hit only coastal regions, they can on occasion wreak havoc far inland before dying out. Many schemes are afoot to 'tame' such fierce storms, either by finding ways to 'steer' a hurricane out to sea away from land, or by somehow cutting off the growth of a baby hurricane before it can rage out of control across the ocean. **(5)** ________, given that all the cogs of the weather machine are interrelated. Hurricanes may cause damage, but a large proportion of the water supply of countries such as Mexico and Japan comes from their rains.

A It could even cut off the vital rainfall over faraway Europe

B But even such seemingly worthwhile endeavours are fraught with dangers

C Farther away from the eye, the swirling mass spreads over a diameter ten times greater

D The eye itself is a region of descending air

E But any precautions are likely to prove inadequate in the face of such fierce winds

F It takes a brave scientist to make investigations in ships or aircraft subjected to such storms

G A hurricane in miniature, a tornado is only 100 to 200 metres in diameter

6 *You are a journalist working for an evening paper. You arrive at the scene of a road accident and make some notes.*

Use your notes, shown below, to write a brief report for your paper. You must use all the words **in the order they appear in the notes.** *You may add words and change the form of words where necessary. There is no need to add any new ideas. Look carefully at the sample sentence which has been done for you.*

a Barnaby Rd blocked today's rush hour head-on collision car lorry.

b After collision lorry → lamp-post (fell, crushed car, Ford Lotus).

c Two ambulances – no one hurt.

d Car driver, J F Blake, lucky escape – saved by crash helmet always wears.

e Keen motorcyclist – says knows important wear helmet riding; thinks important driving too.

f Angry so many accidents Barnaby Rd.

g (Claims 7 last 3 months – lower speed limit.)

h Says someone killed if nothing done.

Accident Chaos in Barnaby Road

a *Barnaby Road was blocked during today's rush hour after a head-on collision between a car and a lorry.*

b ______________________________

c ______________________________

d ______________________________

e ______________________________

f ______________________________

g ______________________________

h ______________________________

TEST FOUR

PAPER 4 LISTENING 35 minutes

SECTION A

*You will hear a television announcer giving details of the evening's viewing on BBC 1 and BBC 2. As you listen, answer questions **1-14** by filling the blanks in the programme schedule. You will hear the piece twice.*

BBC 1		
TIME	PROGRAMME	INFORMATION
6.00	1	
6.45	2	Gives details of the Bradford 3
4	Attwood Chase	
5	Mysterious Realm	Investigates reports of big 6
7	The News	
8	Popscene	

BBC 2		
TIME	PROGRAMME	INFORMATION
9	Sports Review	Reports on damage by 10
7.30	11	Are 12 lurking in our towns?
13	King Lear	Ends at 14

SECTION B

You will hear a student, John, telling a friend about the unexpected events which occurred when he went to get a summer job. For questions **15-30**, *complete the notes using one or more words; you do* **not** *need to write whole sentences.*

Listen carefully as you will hear the piece ONLY ONCE.

John decided to walk from the station to his **15** ______

but he got very **16** ______ . When he put his hand in his

pocket for his **17** ______ he found that it was full

of **18** ______ .

He tried to dry his **19** ______ by hanging it over a

20 ______ but it started to

21 ______ .

He was worried about getting home because his **22** ______

was useless.

Then a man arrived. He was soaked, like John, and he told the woman that his

23 ______ had broken down. He showed her

his **24** ______ , which seemed to have something wrong

with it. He told her to say that he was away on **25** ______

and that John should be given some **26** ______ to cover his

27 ______ . He also said she should take John round the

28 ______ and the

29 ______ and could give him the

30 ______ .

SECTION C

*You will hear an interview in which a radio presenter, Mr Murphy, interviews a politician, Mr Biggs, about Mr Biggs's plans for the local transport system. For questions **31-41**, complete the notes using a few words; you do not need to write full sentences. You will hear the piece **twice**.*

Mr Biggs complains that cars cost a lot to **31** [ ] and **32** [ ]. He says that some people get about just as well **33** [ ]. He recommends introducing frequent **34** [ ] which people could use without **35** [ ].

If people wanted to be picked up at **36** [ ] they would simply have to **37** [ ], but unless they were sick or elderly they would have to **38** [ ].

Mr Murphy thinks people might be offended by his attitude to **39** [ ] but he does not believe other passengers would like to be **40** [ ].

Mr Biggs explains that to get to a place a long way off the bus's route a passenger would have to travel to the **41** [ ] first.

SECTION D

Now look at section D for the last part of the test. You will hear various people describing their reasons for making a journey. TASK ONE lists the reasons. Put them in the order in which you hear them by writing a number from 1–5 in each box. Three boxes will remain empty.

TASK 1

Breaking or enforcing the law	42	
Medical treatment	43	
Getting orders	44	
Going for an interview	45	
Standing for election	46	
Looking after someone	47	
Taking part in a competition	48	
Seeing a foreign country	49	

TASK TWO lists the jobs the people do to earn their living. Put them in the order in which they occur by writing a number from 1–5 in each box. Three boxes will remain empty.

You will hear the series twice.

TASK 2

Teacher	50	
Businessman	51	
Politician	52	
Student	53	
Athlete	54	
Criminal	55	
Secretary	56	
Lawyer	57	

TEST FOUR

PAPER 5 SPEAKING 15 minutes

QUESTION 1 *(candidate 1)*

The examiner will ask you to describe the photograph on page 91 to your partner, who has a photograph which is related to yours in some way.

At the end of one minute the examiner will ask your partner to say what the relationship between your pictures is. You should then try to reach agreement with your partner.

NB: The instructions would not appear on the examination material in the real exam. They would be conveyed orally by the examiner.

QUESTION 1 *(candidate 2)*

The examiner will ask your partner to describe a photograph to you. The photograph on page 95 is related to your partner's in some way.

After one minute you may ask short questions if you wish or find it necessary. The examiner will then ask you to say what the relationship between the photographs is. You should then try to reach agreement with your partner.

QUESTION 2 *(candidate 1)*

The examiner will ask your partner to describe one of the six photographs below to you.

At the end of one minute the examiner will ask you to say which photograph your partner was describing.

QUESTION 2 *(candidate 2)*

The examiner will ask your partner to describe one of the six photographs below to you.

At the end of one minute the examiner will ask you to say which photograph your partner was describing.

QUESTION 3 *(both candidates)*

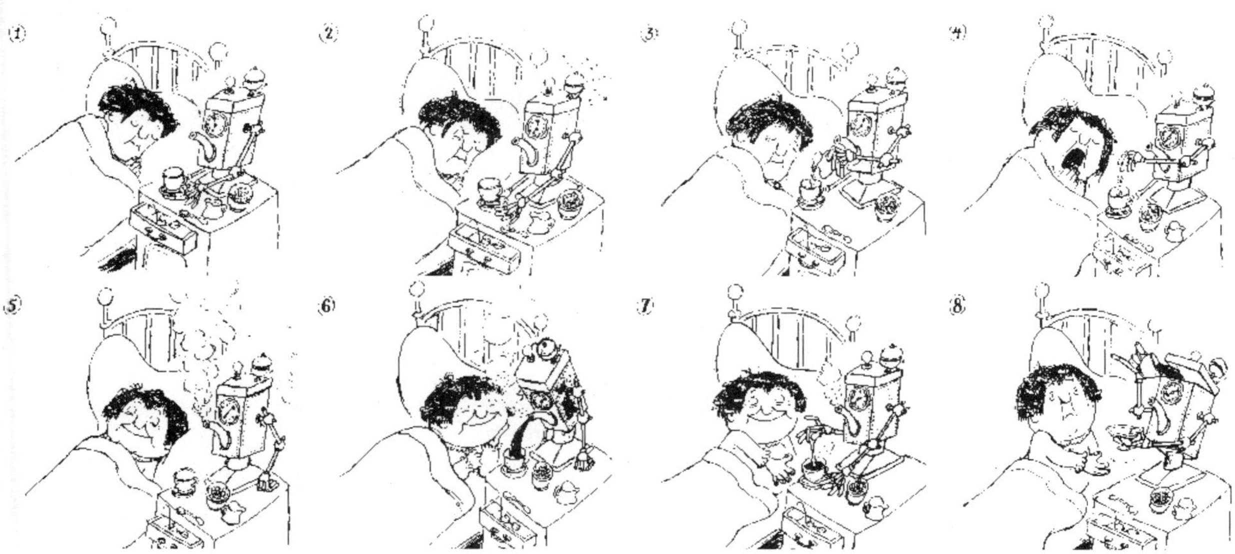

Look at the set of cartoons.

Discuss with your partner what they show and what the artist is trying to say. You must either reach agreement or 'agree to disagree'. Make sure that you understand your partner's opinion. At the end of three minutes you will be asked to report your decision to the examiners, and take part in further discussions.

TEST ONE

PAPER 5 SPEAKING

QUESTION 1 (candidate 1)

The examiner will ask you to describe the photograph below to your partner, who has a photograph which is related to yours in some way.

At the end of one minute the examiner will ask your partner to say what the relationship between your pictures is. You should then try to reach agreement with your partner.

TEST TWO

PAPER 5 SPEAKING

QUESTION 1 (candidate 1)

The examiner will ask you to describe the photograph below to your partner, who has a photograph which is related to yours in some way.

At the end of one minute the examiner will ask your partner to say what the relationship between your pictures is. You should then try to reach agreement with your partner.

TEST THREE

PAPER 5 SPEAKING

QUESTION 1 (candidate 1)

The examiner will ask you to describe the photograph below to your partner, who has a photograph which is related to yours in some way.

At the end of one minute the examiner will ask your partner to say what the relationship between your pictures is. You should then try to reach agreement with your partner.

TEST FOUR

PAPER 5 SPEAKING

QUESTION 1 (candidate 1)

The examiner will ask you to describe the photograph below to your partner, who has a photograph which is related to yours in some way.

At the end of one minute the examiner will ask your partner to say what the relationship between your pictures is. You should then try to reach agreement with your partner.

TEST ONE

PAPER 5 SPEAKING

QUESTION 1 (candidate 2)

The examiner will ask your partner to describe a photograph to you. The photograph below is related to your partner's in some way.

After one minute you may ask short questions if you wish or find it necessary. The examiner will then ask you to say what the relationship between the photographs is. You should then try to reach agreement with your partner.

TEST TWO

PAPER 5 SPEAKING

QUESTION 1 (candidate 2)

The examiner will ask your partner to describe a photograph to you. The photograph below is related to your partner's in some way.

After one minute you may ask short questions if you wish or find it necessary. The examiner will then ask you to say what the relationship between the photographs is. You should then try to reach agreement with your partner.

TEST THREE

PAPER 5 SPEAKING

QUESTION 1 (candidate 2)

The examiner will ask your partner to describe a photograph to you. The photograph below is related to your partner's in some way.

After one minute you may ask short questions if you wish or find it necessary. The examiner will then ask you to say what the relationship between the photographs is. You should then try to reach agreement with your partner.

TEST FOUR

PAPER 5 SPEAKING

QUESTION 1 (candidate 2)

The examiner will ask your partner to describe a photograph to you. The photograph below is related to your partner's in some way.

After one minute you may ask short questions if you wish or find it necessary. The examiner will then ask you to say what the relationship between the photographs is. You should then try to reach agreement with your partner.

LISTENING SCRIPTS

TEST ONE

SECTION A

Look at the railway map and sentences 1-9. You will hear a radio travel bulletin. As you listen you should use the information in the bulletin to complete the sentences. You will hear the piece **twice.**

Good morning. And we start with some news for commuters and long-distance travellers on British Rail's troubled Eastern Region. The area worst affected is the East Anglian sector, centred on Norwich, where the recent gales have caused signal failures and landslides blocking, or partially blocking, a number of lines. In particular, the main line between Norwich and London is blocked near Diss and is closed to all traffic between Norwich and Stowmarket. Passengers travelling to and from Diss are being transported by special coach, while passengers travelling from Norwich to London are being advised to avoid the main line and use the route via Ely and Cambridge, allowing an extra hour for their journeys.

Passengers from Norwich to Ipswich should also take an alternative route, with a change of train at Lowestoft. British Rail say that where passengers have to make extra changes they will do their best to see that connections are ready and waiting.

Now a word for passengers from Ely and Cambridge to Ipswich. British Rail tells us that you should enjoy a normal or near-normal service, though signalling problems – and flooding near Newmarket – may involve certain trains from Cambridge being diverted via Ely. Diverted trains are likely to take an extra 20 or 25 minutes, and passengers to and from Cambridge are advised to make allowance for this.

Lastly, there are problems in the Acle and Cromer areas, affecting services between Norwich and the coastal towns of Yarmouth, Cromer and Sherringham. Some services to Yarmouth will be diverted via Reedham, with a coach service linking Reedham and Acle. Trains from Norwich to the north Norfolk coast will terminate at North Walsham, and passengers will complete their journey by special coach. This will run on a circular route via Sherringham and Cromer, and will pick up passengers wishing to join the train at North Walsham and travel southwards to Wroxham and Norwich.

Now listen to the piece again.

SECTION B

10 *You will hear two people discussing what they need to buy at the start of their holiday. As you listen tick the boxes that correspond to the things that one of the people, John, is expecting to get.*

Listen carefully as you will hear the piece ONLY ONCE.

Chris: For someone who's just arrived on holiday you don't look particularly cheerful, John.

John: I suppose I don't. It's such a problem turning up in a strange town and having to get in food supplies for the week ahead. And not just food – we need all sorts of other things too.

Chris: Well we can go shopping more than once. What are you planning to get for us this time?

John: Well I think we'll need lots of nice cool drinks. I know what it's like in these caravans. The sun beats down on the roof all day and you get really hot. So I think I'll get fruit juice rather than tea or coffee. But I *will* get some milk – to have on our cereal.

Chris: What sort of cereal will you get?

John: Well I know you like cornflakes. But *I* like porridge. So I'll get some of each and we'll both be happy.

Chris: Don't forget we need some bread – I know you like your morning toast.

John: Right. And as well as marmalade I'll get some butter – or rather margarine – to go on it.

Chris: Why not butter?

John: Well I think it might go bad rather quickly in the fridge. Margarine's better in weather like this. After all, we don't even know if the fridge is working properly. Oh! and that reminds me – I'll get some matches. We need them to light the fridge and the cooker. They both run on gas – or I think they do. What about other household things? Oh yes, we'll need some washing up liquid to do the dishes – I know you love lots of washing up – and I'll get a bit of soap for ourselves. And of course we'll need some washing powder to do our clothes.

Chris: Really? It'd be far easier to take them to the launderette. There's one on the campsite.

John: Okay, I'll scrap the washing powder.

Chris: We need a lot more food of course. What about fruit?

John: I was coming to that. Grapes go bad too easily so I'll give them a miss. And tomatoes get squashed too easily.

Chris: Tomatoes get squashed too easily? You must be joking. Surely you can bring some tomatoes home without destroying them.

John: Oh well I'll try. But don't forget I'll be bringing everything home in the rucksack. You know how things get jolted about. Now let me see – I'd better get some other salad things. Can you give me a pencil? I need to write all this lot down . . . . Thanks. Oh it's blunt but never mind.

Chris: What does *that* say? Olives and celery?

John: No, onions and lettuce. We both like spring onions. But I won't bother with cooked beetroot. It always leaks and turns the rest of the shopping purple. I'll get it raw and we'll cook it ourselves. Incidentally, it turns salad cream bright green.

Chris: Oh I never knew that . . . Oh by the way – tinned beans are good.

John: What? For salads?

Chris: Yes – *and* for breakfast, lunch, tea, supper . . . beans on toast.

John: I'm not so sure. I think I'd like a change this year. What about tinned spaghetti in tomato sauce? And I'll tell you what – I'll get some cheese to grate and sprinkle over the top.

Chris: Ok that'll do.

John: By the way – I always like something to nibble. It's a case of making a choice because I tend to be greedy. They all appeal to me – toffees, nuts, chocolate, the lot.

Chris: Yes, and look how many sweets you sucked on holiday last year.

John: Oh come on, be fair – I was sucking those because of my throat.

Chris: Well get some proper throat sweets this time. And try to do without all the other fattening things.

John: Oh well, I'll just get throat sweets and peanuts – and one other thing – let me write it down before I forget . . . , Chewing gum and . . .

Chris: What's that you're writing? Oh come on, John, I think it's ridiculous! You say you can't carry tomatoes – and then you think you can carry crisps. They'd be in crumbs by the time you got them here in your rucksack.

John: Ok, well I'll eat them on the way home. So what shall I have instead of crisps for when I'm at home? I know – I'll get some sticks of rock – and any left over we can give to our friends when we get back home.

Chris: Fat chance of that!

SECTION C

You will hear a doctor and a professor speaking in public about how to study successfully. For Questions ***11-28,*** *complete the notes using a few words; you do not need to write full sentences. You will hear the piece* ***twice.***

Dr. Murphy: Good evening, Professor Jenkinson, and welcome to our college forum on really effective study methods. It's encouraging to see that so many new students have come along - obviously eager to make the most of their time at Greyfriars Institute. Oh – perhaps I should introduce myself before we go on. I'm Bill Murphy, one of the doctors at the Student Health Centre.
Now then, Professor Jenkinson, as a professor of education you must have some really good ideas about how best to study.

Prof. Jenkinson: Well they may be good but they're also quite simple. I think I'd ask the young people in the audience the following question: Have you ever considered how much of your life is made up of habit? You have habits of sleeping, of waking, of getting out of bed, of washing and dressing, of eating and drinking, and so on. Indeed, if a considerable part of our lives were not reduced to the level of automatic action we should be unable to apply ourselves to the more demanding tasks of life.

Dr. Murphy: So to put it in really simple terms, you mean habit saves effort.

Prof. Jenkinson: Yes, that's right, and it saves our energies for the things that need our full attention – like successful study.

Dr. Murphy: But wouldn't you say that habit comes into study too?

Prof. Jenkinson: Oh yes indeed. We can even automate some of our study activities. Good habits of study are most important.

Dr. Murphy: Good habits of study? What does that really mean in practice?

Prof. Jenkinson: Well, I think we can group them under three headings: Place-habits, time-habits and health-habits. Let me start by saying a little about good place-habits. My advice is this: As far as possible, study in one definite location: your room in lodgings or hall of residence, or a corner of a library – at any rate a quiet place.

Dr. Murphy: Does it *have* to be a quiet place? You see, some of the students who come to the Health Centre – complaining, perhaps of hearing troubles – assure me that having their Walkmans playing in their ears really does do wonders for their concentration—even if it's bad in other respects.

Prof. Jenkinson: Well I'd advise against it myself. I think if you use a Walkman your concentration can slip and you don't even notice what's happened – you get so absorbed in the music.

Dr. Murphy: Fine. So can you tell us some more about studying in the right place?

Prof. Jenkinson: Well I'd say as far as possible you should reserve a table or desk for study, since the comfort of an armchair is not conducive to prolonged periods of peak alertness. Remove all distracting elements from your desk (that letter or newspaper from home, that photograph of a far-away loved one, that tempting new novel, even the books you are not studying at the moment). And it's a good thing to prepare your study table each night with pencils, ink, paper and the books you will need, so that you can get down to work with the minimum delay.

Dr. Murphy: Forgive me, Professor, but isn't this going a little too far? You see, students come to me at the Health Centre really quite stewed up over work . . .

Prof. Jenkinson: Stewed up? I don't think I know what that means.

Dr. Murphy: Well really on edge – not sleeping and so on. Surely worrying about the next day's work – last thing at night – is a recipe for insomnia.

Prof. Jenkinson: Well you have a point. Some students might do better to leave their preparations until they wake up bright and refreshed on the following day. But may I say this: The habit of doing things in good time will save a lot of stress in the long run. I'm sure the students who come to you are the ones, mostly, who've left things until the last minute – essays, vital reading and everything. If those students had only worked systematically right from the start of their studies they'd be coping much better later on.

Dr. Murphy: So consider getting your workplace ready the night before. Now then, I think we'd better move on. What about time-habits, Professor Jenkinson?

Prof. Jenkinson: Yes it's very simple: Decide which nights of the week and which hours of these nights you are to devote to study and stick to them. Let your friends know when your working hours are, and do not let them disturb you. If you are sharing a study or study-bedroom with another student or students come to some arrangement – respect each other's study hours. It's best, of course, if all of you buckle down to study at just the same time.

Dr. Murphy: Yes, I'm sure that's right, Professor. But what about the ideal *length* of a study period?

Prof. Jenkinson: Well that's a difficult one I must say. It shouldn't be too short or it will be over before you've got properly 'warmed up'; and it shouldn't be too long – because that would just leave you bored and fatigued.

Dr. Murphy: Yes, my personal view is that you can't do much in less than an hour.

Prof. Jenkinson: Well half-hour periods *can* be used – especially for jobs like background reading, looking up references, skimming through a chapter to get its general plan.

Dr. Murphy: But what's your idea of a proper, full-scale study period?

Prof. Jenkinson: A three-hour period with one or two short breaks is probably a reasonable period to study a slice of a textbook.

Dr. Murphy: And what's the best time of day for study?

Prof. Jenkinson: Well, people vary. But I'd say this: Always reserve the time when you personally are at your freshest for the most difficult part of your work or for some creative activity like essay-writing or problem-solving.

Dr Murphy: Perhaps it's time to move on to the subject of health-habits now.

Prof. Jenkinson: Yes, that's true. I can see the clock ticking away on the wall and I'm sure no one wants to be kept too long. But just one other thing about the time we give to our various study activities. On the whole I've warned against making our study periods excessively brief. As I've said, there *are* things we can usefully do in half an hour or even less. I've given some examples and there's one more I'd like to add to the list: If you're learning something by heart the study period should be short – 20 minutes or so, though it may perhaps form part of a longer swotting session.

Dr. Murphy: Yes, little and often, that's the secret of learning by heart.

Prof. Jenkinson: Incidentally, Doctor, I should imagine that *you're* the better person to say a few words about the health habits students should try to acquire.

Dr. Murphy: Well it's common sense really. Eight hours' sleep a night – that's important. And exercise: if you don't play a game or indulge in gymnastics at least do some brisk walking every day. Even if you spend 56 hours a week in sleep, 15 to 20 hours at classes and 30 to 40 hours at your books – well you still have 30 to 40 per cent of your week left for routine chores and leisure and recreational activities.

Prof. Jenkinson: Yes, that's very true. In the long run, of course, what matters is not how much time you spend on study but *how well* you study. The better you organise your study time the more time you'll have left for healthy recreation.

Dr. Murphy: Well that's a cheerful note to end on. So thank you Professor – and thank you all for coming along and listening so attentively.

Now listen to the piece again.

SECTION D

Now look at section D for the last part of the test. You will hear various people talking about how they spend their evenings.

TASK ONE lists their pastimes or activities. Put them in the order in which you hear them by writing a number from 1–5 in each box. Three boxes will remain empty.

TASK TWO lists the people you hear speaking in the five extracts. Put the speakers in the order in which you hear them by writing a number from 1–5 in each box. Three boxes will remain empty.

You will hear the series twice.

Yes, after spending a day at the wheel I need some exercise during the evening. My work does give me a little exercise – putting luggage into the boot and taking it out again – that sort of thing. But I still enjoy my evening dip. I'm not very fast but at least I can get from end to end.

In the evening I like to see how fast my legs can carry me. They don't get to do much in the daytime. Sitting at the till and working my fingers isn't a very healthy life. But after hours I can sometimes manage an 8-minute mile, which isn't bad for a person of my age.

For me it's a case of more of the same. I'm my own boss you see, delivering messages, urgent letters and so on. I use my bike – it's the fastest way to get round the city. In the evening I simply head for the countryside, away from all the traffic and fumes. But it's speed and freedom I want, not birdsong!

It's back breaking work: digging, raking, bending over all the while. By the evening I've had enough in the way of exercise. Just leave me alone and let me watch my favourite programme.

I like my work but it's very exacting. I have to get everything perfectly right – the light, the shade, the overall composition and layout. Oddly enough, I still have a brush in my hand in the evening. I need the extra money, you see; but at least people's walls and ceilings don't need quite so much care. I mustn't get drips on the carpet, though!

Now listen to the series again.

TEST TWO

SECTION A

*You will hear someone describing the view from a balcony in a city centre. As you listen complete sentences **1–12**. You will hear the piece **twice**.*

Now then, can you all see clearly?

I want you to look out over the city. This is an excellent vantage point for seeing a number of major buildings, and I'll try to point out some of the really important ones for you. Let's start in the north – that means looking to the left, of course. I think you can probably make out a factory chimney with wooded hillsides beyond. Can you see it? Well that's the chimney of Salt's Mill, built last century. And clustered round the mill, or at least on three sides, are the cottages Sir Titus built for his workers. Perhaps some of you can see the canal, the river and the railway, all of which served the mill, in its heyday, in different ways.

Now then, look a little less sharply to the left. Look in a more north easterly direction. Perhaps you can see the football ground – that should be easy to recognise because the floodlights, for some strange reason, are blazing away despite the bright sunlight. Ok, now look beyond it, and perhaps you can see the city's airport. As a matter of fact, there's a plane just coming in to land – it's over – it appears to be over – the airport control tower right now.

And looking a little more to the east – in fact almost straight ahead of us now– you can see the Cathedral. An ugly sight, so many visitors seem to think, but well worth a visit for the beautiful stained glass windows. Of course they'll really glow with the sunlight on a day like this. As a matter of fact, if you went this lunchtime you'd have the bonus of a string quartet. There's music in the Cathedral everyday at lunchtime – it's worth remembering that.

Now look slightly to your right and you'll see the shopping centre and the city's huge new transport terminal. Some say it takes up too much room and could do with cutting down to size. Anyway, there it is. And beyond – if the sun on the terminal roof isn't dazzling you – you can probably make out our lovely new mosque; a wonderful structure – purpose-built and intensely beautiful, especially close up.

Now then, turning to your right and looking directly southwards you can see the new industrial zone and the newly-built spur from the motorway. You can also see new housing estates and blocks of flats. This is one of the very few cities to have gone on building blocks of flats into the 1990s. Of course, lessons have been learned following the rapid decay and demolition of the blocks of flats that were put up during the 1960s. You can probably see the conservatories built on balconies and the rooftop gardens. As a matter of fact I live in one of those blocks myself and I wouldn't change it for anything.

Well thank you, ladies and gentlemen, and now . . .

Now listen to the piece again..

SECTION B

*You will hear two people discussing the changes that have been made to a house. For questions **13-23** fill in the blank spaces in the table.*

Listen carefully as you will hear the piece ONLY ONCE.

Mary: Well, John, you've really changed your house out of all recognition; there's hardly a single room left unaltered.

John: That's perfectly true. This conservatory where we're standing now – you remember what it was before?

Mary: Well, I can't really remember; but looking around me I see some signs of water pipes . . . and there's a tap on the wall over there. So I suppose this was once . . .

John: Yes, that's right. And the sink was just there – near where you're standing. Of course now that it's a conservatory – or call it a sun lounge if you like – I use the tap to get water for my indoor plants.

Mary: Those nasturtiums certainly look really grand.

John: That's right – the flowers are marvellous – and we actually eat the leaves and the seeds. Ok, so you've seen what we've done to the *old* kitchen; now let me take you through to the new one. Mind the steps.

Mary: Right. Ah yes, I remember – this was the dining room last time I came. So the next room must be the dining room now. But in that case what do you do for a lounge?

John: We've built a new one – there, where the oak tree and pond used to be.

Mary: Really, how lovely – though isn't it rather a shame to lose part of your garden?

John: You *could* say that – but it's a single storey extension – and we've made the flat roof into a garden.

Mary: Roof gardens – oh I do like those! But how do you get to it?

John: Well you remember the smallest bedroom – where Jane used to sleep? Well she's left home now and I use it as a billiard room. Anyway I've knocked a hole in the wall and put french windows in and a balcony – so when it's fine we can step straight out and bask in the sun. Just above where we're standing now. It's a splendid arrangement – except that the room's rather small for snooker; I keep on putting my cue through the glass.

Mary: So how many bedrooms have you got now?

John: Well we've still got three. You remember the biggest bedroom – and the one next door? Well, they're unchanged. And do you remember I kept on saying that cars were filthy things and ought to be scrapped? Well, we've done away with our car and turned the garage into a bedroom. So we're back to three. And I'll tell you what else we've done. You know the little porch that linked the garage and the house? Well, that's still there – it's one of the things we haven't changed – and we use it to get to the bedroom, of course. Well just behind it we used to have the pantry and washroom – which were always untidy. Well we've tiled it and fitted it up with the latest plumbing. If you stay with us long I hope you'll be taking a shower there.

Mary: So this brand new bedroom – it's all very well but don't you need a pantry, washroom, laundry room or whatever you call it?

John: Well, we've plenty of food cupboards in the kitchen. And as for all the washing equipment we've turned the tool shed into a laundry.

Mary: My goodness – what a lot of changes!

John: And the children's playroom – now they've left home – is where we have our instruments and our evening concerts. Why not come along and see my brand new harpsichord?

Mary: A music room . . . a harpsichord . . . It sounds as though you've come into money.

John: Oh no, not at all – it's just that we're getting the benefits of having no car – and no children to feed.

SECTION C

*You will hear a series of questions and answers to do with money. For questions **24–35**, complete the notes using a few words; you do **not** need to write full sentences. You will hear the piece **twice.***

Financial advisor: Well thank you, ladies and gentlemen. Thanks very much for your kind applause. I hope you've enjoyed my talk on money management and have found it helpful. But money management means different things to different people. That's because we all have our own particular needs that have to be met and catered for. A young milkman's needs are likely to be quite different from those of, say, a middle-aged teacher or a doctor about to give up his practice. That's why I always finish these talks by inviting questions. So fire away. Who'll start us off? Yes – the gentlemen in the – er – purple coat.

Rock musician: I play in a rock band and travel the length and breadth of Britain with all my gear – electric guitars, amps and so forth. What advice would you give on how to insure it? It must be worth a couple of grand.

Advisor: Yes, I see – about two thousand pounds. Well I'd go along to a good insurance broker. There's probably quite a few in your local area.
And do make it clear that you tour with these things and use them in a professional capacity. Your policy will cost you more – but you'll have to disclose it, otherwise you won't be probably insured.
Yes – the lady over there at the back on the right, with the white hair.

Middle-aged lady: Thank you. I'm a teacher, and as you can probably gather from my white hair I'm drawing near to retirement age. Now the question I want to ask is this: Do you recommend Premium Bonds for someone – not especially well off – at my particular time of life?

Advisor: I expect nearly everyone here is familiar with Premium Bonds. You buy them for a few pounds each – you can hold up to thousands of pounds worth in total – and can quickly convert them back to cash if you wish to do so. Your investment does not earn regular interest but you do get the chance of a big cash payout every month. The lucky few are chosen at random – some people seem to win all the time; others never win at all. I think Bonds are really for the younger age-range – people who can afford to dream for years on end. I think for someone approaching retirement my advice would be to cash your Bonds. Treat yourself with some of the money and with what's left find a new investment that pays monthly income you can really rely on.

The gentleman in the brown blazer . . .

Plumber: I'm 45 years old and I'm a self-employed plumber. Being self-employed I ought to be able to manage money but I have a problem with credit cards. I use them too much then I have to pay interest on the money I owe. Do you think I should give my credit card up?

Advisor: On the contrary, I'd advise you to have two or three different cards. Spread your spending over them all. Then hopefully you can clear the debt on one card a month and only pay interest on the rest. But mind you don't increase your borrowing – that would be most unfortunate.
Now then – the young gentleman there at the front. Speak up for us, please.

Boy: I get £2 pocket money every week. What's the best way for me to save up for Christmas?

Advisor: What a sensible question. Well I'd advise you to open a savings account at your local post office. Perhaps you can save £1 a week. Then by Christmas you'll have enough – how much will that be? about £45 – to treat your family really well. Incidentally if you're planning for Christmas at this early stage you're obviously very wise with your money. Carry on like that and you'll make a fortune.
Now then madam . . .

Old lady: How can I keep my money safe? I prefer to keep it under my bed – in a little box – but I'm so afraid of being robbed. There are so many burglars nowadays.

Advisor: May I ask, madam – has something happened to put you off banks?

Old lady: Well yes, I used to work in one. One night I remember the bank was robbed. People's money – their precious goods and documents – they were never seen again you know.

Advisor: Well I can understand how you feel. But surely customers get their money refunded to them – and compensation for all their valuables.

Old lady: Well yes, I dare say the bank was insured.

Advisor: Frankly, I think you'd be well advised to put your trust – and your money – in your nearest bank or building society.

Old lady: Perhaps you can send me some details. I live at 17 . . .

Advisor: No please madam – don't tell anyone your address. Not in view of what you've said. That would be really asking for trouble.

Old lady: Oh I see, yes. I'm beginning to understand the risk I'm running. I'll get along to a bank in the morning.

Advisor: Well I don't see any more hands up so I think it's time to close the meeting. Let me just thank you once again for . . .

Now listen to the piece again.

SECTION D

Now look at section D for the last part of the test. You will hear various people describing their problems.

TASK ONE lists the problems. Put them in the order in which you hear them by writing a number from 1-5 in each box. Three boxes will remain empty.

TASK TWO lists the places where the people are. Put the places in the order in which they occur by writing a number from 1-5 in each box. Three boxes will remain empty.

You will hear the series twice.

Well, I was over there – that's right, where the Four Star Extra is – and I think I must have dropped it then. I missed it almost at once but I had to go on to the next big junction before turning back. I wonder whether your mechanic has seen it.

Oh good morning. I wonder whether you can help me. I arrived on the 8.57 from Crewe, but it got in late and the train from Scotland had already gone. Now I just don't know what's happened to her – the aunt who was coming down from Dundee. I feel so bad – I'd *promised* to be here.

And when I turn it on nothing happens – or the sound comes on without the picture. Look I'll try the remote control. Where is it, now? ah yes, by the ashtray. You see? It's the same. Scouring the library for interesting books is all very well – but I do feel lost without it, you know.

It's hard, this couch, so I don't sink into it quite so much. But my bed at home is really soft. It doesn't keep my back so straight and the pain seems to start as I'm falling asleep. I'd love a new bed but I can't afford it. I suppose all you can do is give me something to ease it a bit.

It's all down my back. I was just going under this ladder, you see – when the accident happened. It's *your* shop front that's being painted, and this certainly won't come off my suit.

Now listen to the series again.

TEST THREE

SECTION A

You will hear a tape of a radio broadcast. It describes the past and present uses of sites and buildings in the town of Morley. You will find that most have changed their function over the years. Listen to the recording and answer ***questions 1-10*** *by completing the table. Use no more than three words per answer. You will hear the piece twice.*

As curator of Morley's Museum of Local History I'm obviously a great believer in local institutions, and I'm grateful to our local radio station, Radio Helmsdale, for giving me this five-minute local history spot.

Local history – that means the history of Morley itself. It's amazing to find how much things have changed with the passing of the centuries, and especially during the present century. Look at the children's adventure playground in Crossley Street. Look at its humps, hollows and the rocky slopes children love to climb. All these exciting contours stem from the quarrying which was done at the site – perhaps a few older listeners can remember playing there when it was all for real!

Incidentally, the stone from the quarry was used to build the railway station – that's the one we still use today. There was in fact an earlier one which can still be seen – if you know where to look. Now then, rack your brains and see if you can think where it is . . . I expect you're stumped. There don't seem to be any likely buildings anywhere near the present railway. Well let me surprise you – don't look for the station near the line. Look for it half a mile from the line near the service station on Morley bypass. As the traffic thunders along the road cast your mind back – it requires quite a feat of imagination, I have to admit – and picture the steaming locomotives, belching smoke and crunching their ponderous way from Morley Junction to Winston Green. It's not uncommon for railways, especially branch lines, to be converted to roads, and that's exactly what's happened in this case. And many old stations are now the homes of new and thriving cottage industries. In Morley's case a clothes peg factory has been set up in the booking hall and waiting room, while the office and platform area is now a cafe with outdoor seating. I'd personally rather see locomotives than modern lorries but maybe that's a matter of taste.

Oh – by the way – the signal box that used to control the junction now controls Morley Taxis. It's their office and centre of operations.

Still on the subject of road transport, I wonder whether you can guess what the car and lorry park was in days gone by. The trees provide a useful clue. Not many car parks are studded, as ours is, with beautiful oak trees. Sadly, they do look out of place within their low protective walls, which always seem ready to jump out into the way of any reversing car, as I know to my cost. Those trees, sad to say, are all that remains of the town's central park. In Victorian times people used to stroll in the leafy shade or enjoy a game of croquet on the lawns now covered over with tarmac and waiting cars.

Of course, Morley still does have its open spaces. There's the recently opened recreation ground on the site of the disused cattle market. And the town has a smart new park and gardens on the site of the former railway works.

Behind the park is one of the most unusual banks – so far as building style is concerned – in the whole of England. The windows and bell tower give a clue to its use in days gone by. As you probably know, its former role was taken over by the big new church in Fishmonger's Street. Now the town's main shopping mall, the street was once devoted, as its name suggests, to a single product. But don't be misled by the name of the street which crosses it. Butcher's Street was not full of butchers. In the days when the new town hall was built at its northern end it was named after Ernest Butcher, who was Mayor at the time. The Town Hall stands on the site of Morley's former bridewell, or prison. Nearby, outside the health centre, converted of course from a Victorian school, you can see the stocks where minor offenders were chained for a day or two's public disgrace.

For an unspoilt Victorian building still giving excellent service in its original role you have only to look at our town library in Wardour Street. Incidentally, the library has some excellent archive material on conditions in the former jail, and the Museum of Local History still preserves a number of times from its courtroom and cells. If anything I've said has aroused your interest in local history do please come along and pay us a visit.

Now listen to the piece again.

SECTION B

You will hear someone giving a message over the telephone. As you listen fill in the information for ***questions 11-26.***

Listen carefully as you will hear the piece ONLY ONCE.

Male voice: Hello?

Miss Birch: Hello. Is Mr Wiggins there?

Male voice: No. I'm afraid he's out of the office just at the moment.

Miss Birch: Oh dear. Well I wonder . . . Perhaps you could kindly give him a message.

Male voice: Yes certainly. Who's speaking, please?

Miss Birch: This is Miss Birch from Well-Tuned Autos Ltd.

Male voice: Hold on, please; let me take that down: Miss Birch . . . Well-Tuned Autos . . . Right, so what's the message please?

Miss Birch: Well we have his car. It's been repaired and it's almost ready for him to collect. There's just one problem. The windscreen wipers still don't work and we don't know whether he wants us to go ahead and order them for him. The thing is this . . he told us to put the car right up to a total cost of £200. Well the cost so far is £187, and the windscreen wipers will cost an extra £50. The small electric motors need replacing, you see.

Male voice: Just hold on a minute. Do I need to write all these figures down?

Miss Birch: Well, just say doing the wipers would take the cost to over £200. And we'd like him to give us a ring and indicate whether he wants us to do them or not. I think he knows our number – yes, I'm sure he does. But if he needs the car in a hurry he can come and collect it at any time. We could always do the wipers later.

Male voice: Yes, I think I've got all that.

Miss Birch: There's one other thing . . . We've noticed some rust – out of sight underneath. It's starting to eat its way through the chassis. Now presumably Mr Wiggins doesn't want us to take any action on this. Quite frankly it would cost a fortune – probably more than the car is worth. But I'd be grateful if you could mention it to him. I dare say I'll be there when he comes to collect the car in which case I can point it out. But I'd like you to mention it just in case I've gone to lunch. In that case there would only be our trainee mechanic on hand to speak to Mr Wiggins and he might not think to mention it . . . Well thanks for your help. I hope I've not been taking up too much of your time.

Male voice: Oh not at all. I think I've got your second point. He needs to know about the corrosion but basically . . .

Miss Birch: Well, it means the car's life is limited. Maybe he'll have to scrap it in 18 months instead of three years.

Male voice: Ok, well I've got the gist of that. I'll put the note on Mr Wiggins' desk right now.

Miss Birch: Oh I'm sorry – there *is* one other thing. We've made a slight mistake on Mr Wiggins' bill. We've mixed up the £85 for parts and the £102 for labour costs. The total's right but I think I just ought to mention it. We computerise our bills these days, so we don't make all that many mistakes, but as soon as I saw Mr Wiggins' print-out I knew it was wrong. But I'm not too clever on computers myself so I'd rather stick with the bill we've got than do him a new one. I don't think he'll mind . . . Well anyway, that really is all. So thank you again for all your trouble.

Male voice: Don't mention it. It's a pleasure. Goodbye.

SECTION C

You are going to hear an exchange between two speakers. One, Mr Burkiss, has recently had his car removed from his drive in the night. For ***questions 27-32*** *choose the answer you think fits best by indicating the letter A,* ***B, C****, or* ***D*** *against the number of each question. Give* ***one answer only*** *to each question..*

You will hear the piece ***twice.***

Counsel: Now then, Mr Burkiss . . . When did you first notice that your car had gone?

Mr B: It was when I got up on the Thursday morning. I looked out to see what the weather was doing and my drive was empty.

Counsel: So your car had been in the drive and not in the public road.

Mr B: Well yes, that's right.

Counsel: Had you locked it properly?

Mr B: Well no, as a matter of fact I hadn't. I'd done up the boot but I'd left the doors open. One of the back ones may have been locked but the driver's door was certainly open.

Counsel: Don't you think that was rather careless?

Mr B: Well not exactly. I live in a very quiet district. Not much crime or anything like that.

Counsel: I'd suggest to you, Mr Burkiss, that you were asking for trouble in leaving the door of a brand new car completely unlocked.

Mr B: I'm just not sure. But I like it to be ready for me in the mornings. I sometimes need to make a quick getaway – a hurried breakfast and I have to get out. I know it does sound careless of me. But I've got new security lighting round my house. So if anyone comes prowling at night the lights come on and hopefully scare the person away.

Counsel: And what exactly brings the lights on? What makes them come on?

Mr B: I think they're – what is it – thermo-sensitive. They pick up the warmth of an intruder's body. As a matter of fact, a cat or a dog will bring them on.

Counsel: So the system must have been very expensive. What did it cost? £500? £1000? At all events a fine example of the latest electronic gadgetry. And why did you decide to invest in such sophisticated anti-crime equipment?

Mr B: Well it did cost a lot. But I felt I should have it. There were one or two burglaries along my road. Some of the older houses – with older people. In fact there were break-ins nearly every night last summer. So at the end of the summer – just 6 months ago – I had an electrical firm to rig it all up for me.

Counsel: Do I detect a contradiction, Mr Burkiss? A moment ago you told the court you didn't need to lock your car because your district was free of crime. Now you're saying there's quite a history of burglaries in your neighbourhood. Would you like to tell us which is true?

Mr B: There were burglaries several streets away – the older houses seemed to attract the criminals. I had no cause to think my car was likely to disappear.

Counsel: But you thought things were likely to disappear from your house, Mr Burkiss. Why else should you have installed the lighting? The lights are there to scare away burglars. From your particular house, Mr Burkiss, not from some house elsewhere in the neighbour-hood. So you knew your car was at risk, Mr Burkiss. Don't you think you were asking for trouble?

All right, Mr Burkiss, let me pursue a different line of questioning. Just suppose someome did come along to steal from your premises . . . Just suppose he took a fancy to your car. Now what would happen as he came up your drive?

Mr B: I don't understand.

Counsel: It's night, Mr Burkiss. It's the dead of night. And someone trespasses onto your drive. What will occur?

Mr B: I'm sorry. I really don't . . .

Counsel: All right, let me put it a little more plainly. You've installed expensive security lighting. Someone, some criminal, wanders along your drive at night and sees, perhaps by the light of a street-lamp, the glinting paintwork of your car. A nice new car only two months old. Now what do these lights of yours do at that moment?

Mr B: Well they switch themselves on. Though I didn't see anything on the Wednesday night when my car disappeared. Sometimes the brightness wakes me up. I suppose it depends how deeply I'm sleeping.

Counsel: Ah! So you've had people prowling in the last few months – since the lights were installed.

Mr B: Well yes, that's right – or it might have been dogs.

Counsel: But you've certainly been awakened by your lights coming on. And for all you know there were prowlers actually in your drive.

Mr B: But I didn't see anything when I looked out. Except once or twice a cat or a dog.

Counsel: Well indeed, Mr Burkiss. And after all, the trespassers might already have fled. So you must have felt glad you'd installed such a system. The lights, in fact, help you to sleep more easily, as you did last night. But contrary to all common-sense you chose to leave your car unlocked.

Mr B: It sounds a bit silly. I know it does.

Counsel: More than just silly, Mr Burkiss. Criminal.

Mr B: I don't understand.

Counsel: I think your car was meant to disappear, Mr Burkiss.

Mr B: I still don't understand what you're getting at.

Counsel: You and your brother deny all knowledge of where your car went and who moved it. But you had an insurance claim form ready.

Mr B: I always keep a claim form ready.

Counsel: Why? Are you really such a bad driver? . . . When did you last make a claim against your insurance, Mr Burkiss?

Mr B: Oh I think about 3 years ago. When I scraped my wing in an accident.

Counsel: But you used a new type of form that the company only issued within the last six months. We will hear your broker confirm the fact later.

Mr B: I don't see what you're getting at.

Counsel: I put it to you that you went to your broker and got a form only days or at most a week or two before your car disappeared. I put it to you that you and your brother agreed that he should remove the car – conveniently left unlocked by you. Then you would approach the insurance company, make a claim and share the proceeds . . . Isn't that right?

Mr B: Why certainly not. I . . .

Counsel: I think that's sufficient for now, Mr Burkiss. And that concludes my questioning.

Now listen to the piece again.

SECTION D

Now look at Section D for the last part of the test. You will hear various people talking about winter.

TASK ONE lists the particular things which people are talking about. Indicate the order in which you hear them by writing a number from 1–5 in each box. Three boxes will remain empty.

TASK TWO lists the people you hear speaking in the five extracts. Indicate the order in which you hear them by writing a number from 1–5 in each box. Three boxes will remain empty.

You will hear the series twice.

Elderly woman: Well I get so cold. You see at my age – what with my rheumatism – I just can't move about very much. And with getting so little exercise my circulation is very poor. The best I can do is wear gloves all day – and sit with a nice hot water bottle.

Young mother: It was wonderful. Some years there was snow right up to my knees and my father helped me to make a snowman. One year we made an igloo and slept in it. Let's hope my children can have the same fun one of these days.

Man: I hate it. I just hate the snow and the ice and the fog. I get called out; I have to take someone to the train or the airport. And needless to say I have to get them there on time. But what can I do when my wheels are skidding all over the place? It's twice as much work – I sometimes have to get out and dig – and the fares, of course, are the same as ever.

Man: So think about your tender plants. Some, of course, are more tender than others. Take figs, for example. They're really quite a marginal case. They'll survive outdoors – but only if you tie a good thick wad of straw around the stems. You can also put it on the ground to protect things like rhubarb crowns. Though rhubarb's a very hardy plant and will usually come through the winter unaided.

Shopper 1: They're always so much dearer in winter.
Shopper 2: Yes, that's right. They seem to put up the prices for Christmas.
S 1: It's not just that. It's the state of the ground. Frozen solid half the time.
S 2: Yes I see what you mean. I suppose they just can't lift things like carrots.
S 1: And they can't get at anything under the snow.

Now listen to the series again.

TEST FOUR

SECTION A

You will hear a television announcer giving details of the evening's viewing on BBC 1 and BBC 2. As you listen, answer ***questions 1-14*** *by filling the blanks in the programme schedule. You will hear the piece twice.*

Tonight's viewing on BBC offers something for everyone. For those who are keen on current affairs our coverage starts at six o'clock, with our regular News on BBC 1. Tonight's bulletin features the space mission lift-off from Florida, brought to you live by satellite. The new-style news presentation, which begins this week, offers punchy, up-to-the-moment headlines every ten minutes, interspersed with the longer in-depth coverage of major items from home and abroad. The 45-minute programme, ending with the weather and local news, is followed by this week's edition of Local and National, a programme devoted to regional issues of national importance. Last week we covered local health care; this week we look at preparations for the forthcoming Bradford Festival. In our multi-cultural society any regional festival of ethnic arts is watched with interest far outside its local area, especially in regions, however far-flung, which have corresponding ethnic minorities. The programme will feature visits by Asian representatives from Scotland and the Birmingham area.

Meanwhile, over on BBC 2 we bring you this week's Sports Review. Tonight's programme has a quirky flavour, with a look at the damage being done by moles to the football pitch at Battersea Park – no joke in view of the ruinous cost of maintaining a pitch, even without the extra cost of dealing with subterranean vermin. That's an hour-long programme from half past six to half past seven. Staying on BBC 2 – and the subject of wildlife spreading to urban habitats – you can see 'Fox Corner'. That's the title we've given to this week's edition of Wildlife Review, a half-hour programme that brings you the finest footage from days of patient filming. Or if humour is more to your taste you can spend the half-hour watching Attwood Chase on BBC 1. For those of you who aren't familiar with this new weekly sitcom series I should add that it's won the Eurovision Award for the most original comedy, and has also attracted critical praise and condemnation – in more or less equal measures – for its treatment of the hunting and killing of deer in parts of Scotland.

Stay tuned to BBC 1 and you'll see the final programme in another controversial series, this time one with a factual slant, or at any rate one where it's sometimes hard to disentangle fact and fiction. The series, in case you haven't guessed, is Mysterious Realm. Each programme has been devoted to a penetrating enquiry into one of the strange phenomena for which Britain is famous the world over. This week, to round the series off, we take a look at the huge black cats which are claimed to exist in places as far apart as Dartmoor and the Scottish Highlands. At the end of the programme the studio audience register their belief or disbelief in the phenomenon under discussion; and while their votes are being counted we ask you at home to ring in with your personal verdict. The hour-long programme is extended so that we can bring you the result of both polls between nine and five past. The ten-minute Mid-Evening News is followed, at a quarter past nine, by Popscene – your chance to get 'with it' and wear out your carpet as you dance – or at any rate tap your feet, depending on age and vitality – to the latest sounds from a wide range of groups.

Now let me just backtrack and fill you in with the BBC 2 bill of fare for mid-evening. This consists of a single item: Jill Houghton's celebrated production of Shakespeare's masterpiece *King Lear*, which runs for a full three hours of high drama, ending at eleven. There's just time, before the News, to let you sample Edward Atherton's towering performance as Lear . . .

Now listen to the piece again.

SECTION B

You will hear a student, John, telling a friend about the unexpected events which occurred when he went to get a summer job. For ***questions 15–30****, complete the notes using one or more words; you do* ***not*** *need to write whole sentences. Listen carefully as you will hear the piece* ONLY ONCE.

Jane: How are you, John?
John: Not bad at all. I've been trying for weeks to get myself a summer job, and I finally managed to get one yesterday.
Jane: Did you have to go for an interview?
John: Well I *went* for one, but it didn't exactly work out as expected.
Jane: It all sounds very mysterious.
John: Well, I'll tell you what happened. The job's in a shop and an upstairs office in Burnley town centre. They rang only yesterday morning and called me there for an interview. The journey – I went by train – was very smooth and comfortable. But when I got out at the station it came on to rain. It wasn't much so I thought I'd walk. I didn't have a mac but I couldn't see any buses or taxis, and anyway it was hardly raining, not at first. But then it came on heavily. I tried to hurry but I still had half a mile to go.
Jane: Oh dear, I bet you were getting soaked.
John: Well I made the mistake of sheltering just in front of a shop. The blind was down so there was a nice sheltered patch of pavement to stand on. Everywhere else the roads and the pavements were getting flooded.
Jane: So where's the mistake?
John: I'm coming to that. You see the blind was sagging in the middle under the weight of the water. It was gathering above my head. And then, of course, the material split and you can guess what happened – one minute I was just

a bit wet; the next minute I was standing in a waterfall. It happened so quickly. The water just came down all over me. I put my hand in my pocket to get a handkerchief to mop my eyes; and do you know, my pocket was full of water. And I do mean full. I decided I might as well hurry through the downpour and get to the place. I started off and my shoes had so much water inside that it squirted out with every step.
Oh you can laugh! But when I turned up at the office I just couldn't face the interview. Not in the dreadful state I was in. I went to the desk and told the receptionist what had happened. She was nice but I could see she was nearly laughing. Anyway, I went to the toilet, took off my jacket and tried to wring out some of the water. I checked my pockets and found that my train ticket was in pieces with all the ink washed off. So I looked in my wallet and I only had a £5 note – not enough to pay the fare home, but at least my fiver was in one piece. I came out and found a radiator and tried to get my jacket dry. There was loads of steam coming up, and you know wet clothes tend to smell a bit – well actually this woollen jacket of mine was smelling dreadful. So what could I do? No money, or not enough to get home – and no chance of getting the job I'd come for. Then the door opened – it was still raining very hard outside – and in came a man with a really posh suit, all dripping wet. He went to the desk and spoke to the woman. 'Look at me,' he said, 'I'm soaked to the skin. My car broke down and I had to walk. And look at my shirt – just look what's happened.'

Jane: Yes, go on – what was wrong with his shirt?

John: Well I couldn't see. But I'll tell you something – he was the boss. He told the woman he couldn't possibly interview anyone that afternoon.

Jane: So what happened next?

John: Well this is the good bit. He told the woman that if that young student (meaning me) turned up she was to pay him his expenses. And she was to tell him the manager had been called away on urgent business and take him round the shop and the office. If he seemed happy just give him the job. After all, it was only for 8 or 10 weeks.

Jane: So he never saw you.

John: No I didn't have an interview. He didn't even see me sitting there. I think he had too much water running into his eyes. And you can't see properly with glasses on – not when they're covered with drops of rain.

Jane: So you got the job. And money to get you home as well.

John: That's right. I start work tomorrow. Just wish me luck.

Jane: And good weather too.

SECTION C

You will hear an interview in which a radio presenter, Mr Murphy, interviews a politician, Mr Biggs, about Mr Bigg's plans for the local transport system. For ***questions 31–41****, complete the notes using a few words; you do not need to write full sentences.*

You will hear the piece ***twice****.*

M: Good evening, Mr Biggs, and welcome to the programme. In the limited time available I wonder whether you could outline some of your policies for this town of ours.

B: Certainly. Well, first of all, a lot of your listeners will be tuned in on their car radios as they battle through rush-hour traffic on their way home from work. But I wonder whether they realise how much time they actually spend on their cars. They have to earn money to buy and maintain them – that takes time – and then there's the time they spend at the wheel. If you tot it all up they spend a whole hour for every 4 or 5 miles they travel.

M: Excuse me, Mr Biggs, but could we come to your actual policies?

B: Well certainly, but policies have to be seen in the context of where we are now.

M: And you're saying that in effect we with our cars manage only 4 or 5 miles an hour.

B: Yes indeed. And many people with so-called primitive life-styles elsewhere in the world get along just as well on foot.

M: So what are the policy implications? Rightly or wrongly, your critics say that you want to make the car redundant. But can you really infringe people's liberties and make them take their cars to the scrap-yard.

B: Well listen here I've no plans for banning anything. But I want to make public transport the obvious, efficient option. Let's have a bus on the principal routes every 4 or 5 minutes. And let's make them free.
As for the side-roads, let's have a bus that will call at your house – for a modest fee – within 5 minutes of your phoning for it.

M: Calling buses to your home by telephone? Is that really practicable? Who can you telephone? And how can buses get anywhere and everywhere within 5 minutes? At busy times it would take half an hour to get from a central depot to an address the other side of the city. And think of the cost.

B: But we've thought about these things most carefully. If the city was criss-crossed with bus routes offering a service every 5 minutes there would always be a bus at hand that would just have to deviate a few hundred yards – or should I say metres these days? – down your particular side-street.

M: So the passengers on board would never know where they might get taken or how long their journey was going to be. And you still haven't told us how the drivers would know where they needed to go.

B: Well forgive me but I think the last point is rather an obvious one. Most of our city buses are already radio-controlled. Your phone request would reach the driver within a few seconds. And as for journey time, do please remember that under my scheme our streets would be transformed. With so much traffic transferred to the buses the journey to the city centre – even with a couple of extra calls – would be far quicker than the present rush-hour journey by car.

M: But Mr Biggs, there are so many problems. For example, let me ask you this: If someone's willing to pay a fee to be picked up –

B: Let me just say that I'd waive the fee for the old and disabled–

M: Alright, well let's forget about the fee. But if someone wants to be picked up maybe they'll want to go – on the bus – to some particular destination off the bus route. How would you cope with that?

B: We'd cope with pleasure and ease, Mr Murphy.

M: But would your buses take them to a point which might be several miles off the route?

B: And what's wrong with that? The sick or the elderly have a right to a door-to-door service.

M: But what about everyone else on the bus? Surely it's impossible. We can't have everyone ... well, in effect being hi-jacked by one sick old lady. I know some people might be offended by my attitude. But even compassion for the sick and elderly doesn't justify such a policy.

B: Well let me explain. The bus would normally finish its run to the city centre. Then – with the passenger still on board – it would switch to a different route – one which went near the passenger's destination. That's really no problem.

M: So the wishes of a single person settle where the bus goes next. A lot of people will think the idea is quite absurd.

B: But you take it for granted if you own your own car. Your personal wishes settle where it goes next. Why not the same for public transport?

M: Well I wonder whether these ideals will work in practice. And what about your other policies? Are they equally revolutionary?

B: Well I hope they are. Let me come to the matter of health. As you know the city has just one central hospital . . .

Now listen to the piece again.

SECTION D

Now look at section D for the last part of the test. You will hear various people describing their reason for making a journey.

TASK ONE lists the reasons. Put them in the order in which you hear them by writing a number from 1–5 in each box. Three boxes will remain empty.

TASK TWO lists the jobs the people do to earn their living. Put them in the order in which they occur by writing a number from 1–5 in each box. Three boxes will remain empty.

You will hear the series twice.

I've been finding it hard to complete my studies – because of this trouble I've been having. I can't get the operation at home but my friends have raised the money to send me to Spain – Barcelona.

As a matter of fact I don't want to go on this trip at all. I've so many clients to represent – crime seems very popular these days. But my son, who's 15, seems to be following in my footsteps. He's going for an interview at Berkeley Law School. Well 15's a little bit young to travel alone so I'm tagging along.

Well, you see I've a long summer holiday. All my pupils are on vacation and I thought to myself: why not widen my horizons? There are still some English-speaking countries – quite major ones – that I've never visited in my life. It'll be a change from typing, shorthand and exercise books.

Well you see it's the summer recess. Parliament is very quiet, though the secretaries and some of the members are still at work. But frankly I'm leaving work behind. I'm still young enough to manage a very fast time round the track. And oddly enough any sporting success seems to help me when it comes to elections. So it all fits in with my career.

Well we've really stolen the march on our competitors now – ice creams that don't need refrigeration – warm or cold they keep their shape. The details are under wraps, of course – we don't want our competitors to muscle in. But there'll certainly be a big demand. I'll make my organisation millions on this one trip.

Now listen to the series again.

ANSWER KEY

TEST ONE

PAPER 1 – READING

Questions 1–8

1 E
2 B
3 C
4 D
5 G
6 F
7 H
8 A

Questions 9–13

9 E
10 H
11 C
12 G
13 B

Questions 14–18

14 C
15 A
16 D
17 B
18 B

Questions 19–23

19 B
20 B
21 B
22 B
23 C

Questions 24–45

24 A
25, 26 B, A
27, 28 A, B
29, 30 C, J
31, 32 D, C
33, 34, 35, 36 C, D, J, G
37, 38 C, E
39 G
40, 41 D, C
42 F
43, 44 F, H
45 I

PAPER 3 – ENGLISH IN USE

Section A Question 1

2 B
3 D
4 B
5 A
6 B
7 C
8 C
9 B
10 C

Section A Question 1 (Continued)

11 B
12 D
13 D
14 B
15 A
16 A

Question 2

1 no
2 what
3 giving
4 of
5 where
6 than
7 death
8 of
9 in
10 of
11 to
12 day
13 be
14 use
15 from/through

Section B Question 3

3 a
4 of
5 it
6 ✔
7 you
8 in
9 the
10 for
11 ✔
12 off
13 must
14 ✔
15 and
16 serve
17 either

Question 4

1 Owing to
2 circumstances/problems
3 unavoidable
4 delay
5 power
6 absence
7 priority
8 present
9 inform
10 progress
11 done/completed
12 September
13 despatched
14 apologies
15 trouble/inconvenience

Section C Question 5

1 G
2 D
3 B
4 C
5 F

Question 6

b It's/It is also important to save your receipt – you'll /you will never/you can never be certain a fault isn't/is not going to/will not crop up later. A new table lamp might burst into flames when you try it out!
c Your receipt should say what you bought, where you bought it, when, and how much it cost. If you have to complain, take the product and (the) receipt back to the shop.
d Remember what the law says: it is the shop's duty to put right the fault, not the manufacturer's.
e If they suggest that you should send the product back to the manufacturer, you can refuse.
f If they say they will send it back to the maker, you can ask for an immediate refund.
g If you have serious trouble, keep/stay/be/remain calm and polite. Leave the shop, and write to the head office. Explain your problem in detail, and remember that you have a right to compensation if you have suffered any injury or damage.

PAPER 4 LISTENING

Section A

1 Eastern
2 gales, signal failures, landslips, floods
3 by special coach
4 the main line, go via Ely and Cambridge
5 (using) an alternative route/changing (trains) at Lowestoft
6 there are connections (ready and) waiting
7 20 or 25, they have to go/of diversions via Ely
8 normal (or nearly normal)
9 (North Norfolk) coast, take the coach to North Walsham (and catch the train there)

Section B

Orange juice	Tomatoes
Milk	Spring Onions
Cornflakes	Lettuce
Porridge oats	Beetroot
Bread	Spaghetti
Marmalade	Cheese
Margarine	Throat sweets
Matches	Peanuts
Washing up liquid	Chewing gum
Soap	Crisps

Section C

11 save us effort/trouble/free us to do more demanding things
12 in a fixed/regular place/in the same place every time

Section C (Continued)

13 at a fixed/regular time
14 sleep
15 exercise
16 damages students' hearing/ears/might be bad in some respects
17 concentration
18 go to bed
19 prepare/put pen, ink, etc. on
20 distracting
21 an hour
22 three/3 hours
23 by heart
24 the hardest/most difficult part of their work/essay-writing/problem-solving
25 a/some creative activity
26 brisk/regular walking
27 regular/systematic/well-organised, study for very long periods/how much time students spend studying/on their studies.

Section D

28	2	36	4
29	1	37	5
30	4	38	–
31	–	39	3
32	3	40	–
33	–	41	2
34	5	42	–
35	–	43	1

TEST TWO

PAPER 1 – READING

Questions 1–7

1 G
2 C
3 B
4 A
5 H
6 D
7 F

Questions 8–33

8, 9 A, B
10, 11 A, D
12, 13, 14, 15 A, D, I, K
16 E
17 F
18, 19 G, H
20 B
21, 22 B, H
23, 24 E, C
25, 26 A, B
27, 28 C, E
29 B
30, 31 D, G
32 D
33 H

Questions 34–38

34 B
35 B
36 D
37 B
38 C

Questions 39–44

39 G
40 A
41 C
42 D
43 B
44 E

Questions 45-48

45 B
46 A
47 C
48 C

PAPER 3 – ENGLISH IN USE

Section A Question 1

2 C
3 C
4 B
5 B
6 D
7 B
8 D
9 C

Section A Question 1 (Continued)

10 A
11 C
12 C
13 A
14 B
15 D
16 A

Question 2

1 to
2 that
3 was
4 through/throughout
5 began/started
6 get
7 after
8 until
9 out
10 it
11 who
12 could/should
13 at
14 which
15 member

Section B Question 3

3 no
4 to
5 ✔
6 the
7 them
8 ✔
9 was
10 ✔
11 away
12 still
13 ✔
14 in
15 ✔
16 the
17 of

Question 4

1 boarding
2 live
3 sleep
4 stand
5 are
6 divided
7 one
8 caught
9 fell
10 prove
11 thought
12 came
13 same
14 first
15 most

Section C Question 5

1 B
2 A
3 C
4 G
5 F

Question 6

- **b** I went/travelled by train and it was quick and comfortable.
- **c** There are some good museums in the Kensington area, which I liked very much.
- **d** Do museums interest you or (do they) bore you?
- **e** After I'd been to the museums I found a cheap hotel, but/(al)though I could only afford to stay a single night.
- **f** I'm a student like you, so I have to be careful with money!
- **g** I had my/an evening meal in my room and went to bed early.
- **h** Next morning I called at/went to/visited the Post Office, so I could send (some/a few) postcards.
- **i** I spent the afternoon sightseeing, and in the evening went/travelled by bus to the station to get/catch/take the train home.

PAPER 4 – LISTENING

Section A

1 wooded hillsides
2 cottages
3 there is bright sunlight/it is daytime
4 there is a plane coming in to land
5 ugly
6 music
7, 8 shopping centre, transport terminal
9 the sun might be dazzling them/too bright
10 blocks of flats
11 gardens
12 roofs

Section B

13 kitchen
14 dining room
15 lounge
16 lounge
17 billiard room
18 bedroom
19 bedroom
20 porch
21 shower

Section B (Continued)

22 laundry
23 music room

Section C

24 different people have different needs
25 tours/travels
26 professional
27 teacher
28 young(er)
29 find a new investment
30 give up his credit card
31 2 or 3/two or three
32 45 weeks
33 buy presents for his family
34 in a box/under her bed
35 she gives (him) her address

Section D

36	2	44	1
37	1	45	–
38	–	46	2
39	4	47	4
40	–	48	3
41	5	49	5
42	3	50	–
43	–	51	–

TEST THREE

PAPER 1 – READING

Questions 1–7

1 B
2 H
3 E
4 C
5 D
6 F
7 A

Questions 8–13

8 B
9 A
10 E
11 D
12 I
13 H

Questions 14–18

14 B
15 A
16 B
17 A
18 B

Questions 19–35

19, 20, 21 J, C, E
22 G
23 A
24 B
25 D
26, 27 H, N
28, 28, 30, 31 K, H, M, N
32, 33 L, L
34, 35 I, M

Questions 36–40

36 D
37 F
38 C
39 G
40 A

Questions 41–45

41 D
42 A
43 C
44 A
45 B

PAPER 3 – ENGLISH IN USE

Section A Question 1

2 C
3 D
4 D
5 A
6 A
7 D
8 A
9 B
10 D
11 A
12 D
13 C
14 B
15 A
16 B

Question 2

1 escape
2 your/the
3 might/may
4 not
5 has
6 could/may/might
7 of
8 well
9 Make/Take
10 going
11 all/everything
12 off
13 sure
14 been
15 closed/shut

Section B Question 3

3 it
4 to
5 up
6 ✔
7 ✔
8 ahead
9 ✔
10 ✔
11 the
12 them
13 but
14 ✔
15 a

Question 4

1 regret
2 satisfied
3 standard/quality
4 recent
5 applied
6 result
7 previous
8 visible
9 addition
10 unacceptable/unsightly
11 therefore
12 rectify/correct
13 fortnight/two weeks
14 Failing
15 obliged/forced
16 expense

Section C Question 5

1 G
2 F
3 D
4 E
5 B

Question 6

b He wants to know how to get to the market. Should he use in his car, or has yours been repaired?/have you had yours repaired?
c Also, he asks what time you start and finish? Will/Do you close early if it's wet?/Will it finish early?
d He can donate an old bike/can he donate his old bike?, which is (rather/a bit) squeaky/It's a bit squeaky, but the brakes are good.
e If his car is not needed, he can ride it here on Saturday.

Question 6 (Continued)

f He's really keen, and thinks the stall will be a great success.
g He's worried about 2 helpers will not be enough. He hopes there'll be hundreds of customers.
h Can Peter help?/He wonders if Peter can/could help/Do you want Peter to help?. He's very strong and can/could carry a lot/plenty of things
i If Peter helps/If Peter is there, we'll have no trouble with thieves (who/they are usually a serious problem at markets).

PAPER 4 – LISTENING

Section A

1 Adventure playground
2 Railway station
3 Railway
4 Car park
5 Cattle market
6 Railway works
7 Bank
8 Town Hall
9 Health centre
10 Library

Section B

11 windscreen wipers
12 wipers
13 £200
14 in a hurry
15 rust
16 under
17 a fortune

Section B (Continued)

18 mention it
19 lunch
20 trainee (mechanic)
21 shorten the life
22 18 months
23 parts
24 labour
25 total
26 computer

Section C

27 B
28 B
29 C
30 B
31 B
32 A

Section D

33 –
34 1
35 3
36 4
37 2
38 –
39 5
40 –
41 3
42 –
43 1
44 2
45 5
46 4
47 –
48 –

TEST FOUR

PAPER 1 – READING

Questions 1–7

1 B
2 F
3 C
4 A
5 G
6 D
7 E

Questions 8–15

8 D
9 A
10 A
11 C
12 B
13 D
14 D
15 D

Questions 16–32

16, 17, 18 D, H, F
19 H
20, 21 E, D
22, 23 A, C
24 G
25 A
26, 27 F, H
28, 29 J, H
30 I
31, 32 D, B

Questions 33–37

33 B
34 H
35 E
36 D
37 F

Questions 38–46

38, 39, 40 I, J, K
41, 42 I, L
43, 44 M, O
45 N
46 M

PAPER 3 – ENGLISH IN USE

Section A Question 1

2 B
3 D
4 A
5 C
6 D
7 B
8 B
9 B
10 B
11 C
12 A
13 C
14 A
15 D
16 D

Question 2

1 into
2 during/lasting/throughout/over
3 involve
4 by
5 then
6 have
7 in
8 with
9 not
10 each
11 to
12 of
13 who
14 above
15 on

Section B Question 3

3 ✔
4 it
5 to
6 along
7 ✔
8 in
9 and
10 ✔
11 the
12 ✔
13 ✔
14 far
15 on

Question 4

1 contacted
2 an attempt/order
3 demonstration
4 However/Unfortunately
5 cannot
6 present
7 tells
8 recently
9 According
10 appreciate/welcome
11 discount
12 both
13 existing
14 prefer
15 urgency
16 action/steps

Section C Question 5

1 F
2 D
3 C
4 E
5 B

Question 6

b After the collision the lorry struck/hit a lamp-post, which fell and crushed the car, a Ford Lotus.
c Two ambulances arrived (on the scene)/ were called, but no one was hurt.
d Car driver J F Blake had a lucky escape. He was saved by the crash helmet he always wears.
e He is a keen motorcyclist, and says he knows how important it is to wear a helmet while riding; he thinks it's important for/when driving, too.
f He is angry that there are so many accidents/so many accidents happen in Barnaby Road.
g (He claims that there have been 7 in the last 3 months. They should lower the speed limit/Why don't they lower the speed limit?)

h He says someone will be killed if nothing is done.

PAPER 4 – LISTENING

Section A

1 News
2 Local and National
3 Festival
4 7.30
5 8.00
6 black cats
7 9.05
8 9.15
9 6.30
10 moles
11 Fox Corner
12 foxes/wild animals
13 8.00
14 11.00

Section B

15 interview
16 wet
17 handkerchief
18 water
19 jacket
20 radiator
21 smell
22 ticket
23 car
24 shirt
25 business
26 money
27 expenses
28 shop
29 office
30 job

Section C

31 buy
32 maintain
33 on foot
34 buses
35 paying
36 home
37 phone (for a bus)
38 pay
39 the sick and elderly
40 hi-jacked/taken out of their way
41 city centre

Section D

42 –
43 1
44 5
45 –
46 –
47 2
48 4
49 3
50 3
51 5
52 4
53 1
54 –
55 –
56 –
57 2

PAPER 5 QUESTION 1

(Suggested answers)

TEST ONE

The relationship between these two photos is the emotion shown, that of anger or frustration.

TEST TWO

The relationship between these two photos is the environment, the people, and the situation, i.e. it is the same event, but shown at the beginning and at the end of the race/lap.

TEST THREE

The relationship between these two photos involves the same person on similar formal occasions, receiving or having received flowers.

TEST FOUR

The relationship between these two photos is that of an action sequence, one following the other.

ISBN 0-435-29484-9

9 780435 294847